RESULTS MANAGEMENT

Effective People Management to Achieve Excellent Results

RESULTS MANAGEMENT

Effective People Management to Achieve Excellent Results

Ong Teong Wan

WILEY

John Wiley & Sons (Asia) Pte. Ltd.

Other Wiley Editorial Offices

John Wiley & Sons, 111 River Street, Hoboken, NJ 07030, USA
John Wiley & Sons, The Atrium, Southern Gate, Chichester, West Sussex, P019 8SQ, United Kingdom
John Wiley & Sons (Canada) Ltd., 5353 Dundas Street West, Suite 400, Toronto, Ontario, M9B 6HB, Canada
John Wiley & Sons Australia Ltd, 42 McDougall Street, Milton, Queensland 4064, Australia
Wiley-VCH, Boschstrasse 12, D-69469 Weinheim, Germany

Library of Congress Cataloging-in-Publication Data

ISBN 978-0-470-82414-6

Typeset in 11/13pt New-Baskerville by Thomson Digital
Printed in Singapore by International Press Softcom Limited

10 9 8 7 6 5 4 3 2 1

DEDICATION

To my wife, Geck Luan; my sons, Yu En and Yu Ee; my daughter-in-law, Grace; and my sister, Sally Chew; for their faith in me and for prompting me to leave something for posterity.

To Emeritus Professor You Poh Seng, former Executive Director of the Singapore Institute of Management, who appointed me in 1984 to pioneer corporate training as another service, after he had developed the Institute as an eminent institution providing management education for working adults. It was my years of work in corporate training at the Singapore Institute of Management that enabled me to learn concepts and develop applications that are useful to practicing managers.

CONTENTS

Acknowledgments ix

A note to the reader xi

Foreword xiii

Preface xv

Introduction xix

1 Overview: The Results-Management System
Achieving results through and with people 1

2 Performance Measurement
Anything measured gets done. Anything measured gets improved 11

3 Performance Management and Review
Managing for commitment, not just for compliance 39

4 Performance Appraisal
A summative evaluation of results achieved 93

5 Compensation System
Paying for the job. Paying market rates. Paying for performance 111

6 Talent-Management System
Placing the right talent in the right place at the right time 125

7 Implementing the Results-Management System
Any system is only as good as its implementation 149

Index 161

ACKNOWLEDGMENTS

To Ms. Jolynn Chow of BeyondWords Training and Consultancy, who did the illustrations and trimmed my long and unwieldy sentences to make them readable and comprehensible for editing. Without her able and professional assistance in business writing, coupled with infinite patience, this book would not have been completed.

To copy editor John Owen, who painstakingly shaped and pruned the whole manuscript into a convenient and readable form for the reader.

To my training workshop participants of all nationalities, from different organizations and levels of management, who have contributed so richly to my own learning and who have encouraged me to commit this to print for future generations of managers.

Last, but not least, to my relatives, corporate clients, close friends and associates who have suggested various titles culminating in one that encapsulates what all individual managers and organizations aspire to do well—manage for results.

A NOTE TO THE READER

Results Management is written for practicing managers who want to enhance the productivity of those under their charge. It translates basic management concepts into practice for the busy line manager who wants to learn from other managers how to be more efficient and effective in achieving results through and with people.

It is based on the real-life managing experiences and insights of many line managers who have attended the author's training workshops on managing for results. The reader is taken inside a fictional large company (Resu Co.) that is representative of most companies selling products or services to customers.

The author, as workshop leader, shares with the reader how he facilitates the training workshops on aspects of the results-management system. The reader is also an observer at the workshops listening to what the participants are saying as they learn how to apply the critical concepts and processes needed to implement a results-management system. These concepts and processes include strategic focus; functional linkages; performance expectations, measurement, management, and appraisal; assessment of potential; compensation; and talent management.

At each training session, participants comprising managers and directors from human resources, production, sales, marketing finance, facilities, IT, and engineering are presented with familiar situations related to the management concepts and practices within the results-management system. They are invited to share their understanding and past approaches to the topic. The workshop leader consolidates their observations and responses, and uses these to introduce new perspectives to the topic under discussion.

The participants' comments and perspectives are based on the typical responses the author has come across in his training programs. They represent a mix of key operational and support personnel who learn fast and are fairly receptive to new ideas.

The following are the key personnel in the company who, once convinced of its merits, will be responsible for implementing the results-management system. Their job designations indicate the perspectives they take during the training workshops. They are either more results-oriented or people-oriented, or both, according to their educational background and work experience. The results-management system requires people to be both results-focused and people-oriented.

Henry: Human Resources Director
Tracy: Training Manager
Ravi: Recruitment Manager
Beatrice: Compensation and Benefits Manager
Frank: Finance Director
Paul: Production Director
Eugene: Engineering (QA) Manager
Martin: Marketing Director
Sally: Sales Manager
Felix: Facilities Manager
Imran: IT Manager

FOREWORD

It is my pleasure to write this foreword. This is a topic dear to my heart. Perhaps I should say it addresses one of the most vexing dilemmas in my work life as a leader and manager.

How do you move your organization forward, keeping your employees positive, committed and focused on continuous improvement? An effective manager needs to identify areas for improvement, to have them understood, accepted and implemented with zest. This is an ideal state. But what is the real state in most organizations?

I've supervised units at two universities in the United States for more than 30 years. The annual performance evaluations happen in the last quarter of the year when we are involved in the budgeting process for the next year and in the final rush of student recruitment. The performance evaluation process disrupts the positive energy developed with staff during the year and worse; I suspect no one at senior levels has time to really read the evaluations and the forms thoroughly.

In the end, salary is really the most important symbol of achievement to the employee – the percentage increase is really determined by a gross ranking of employees by the supervisor.

In a rush, the percentage increase is determined without effective communication between senior managers and line managers. Many factors impacting on performance and results fail to come into play in the process.

More often than not, the employee gets a decent raise, but is perturbed by a few words pointing out areas for improvement, written perhaps in a rush, that irritate more than motivate. One result of this is an employee may react by disagreeing with much of the evaluation or ask for examples, putting the manager in a defensive position. Alternatively, he or she may act as if any negative feedback does not matter and will harbor strong feelings about fairness. Some individuals who are too reticent to speak up due to shyness or cultural norms are clearly hurt in this process because supervisors may respond to assertive staff members more.

It is often said that people in business schools ''can teach but cannot do.'' I have a hunch too that many people in businesses also read and think, but seldom do. We have yet to develop a good system that connects corporate strategy and measurement at the operational level with performance management, evaluation and an equitable reward determination process based on real performance results.

Let's hope this pragmatic book and the ideas in it can invigorate some organizations to re-look at the way individual performers are measured and managed in a supportive systematic way to avoid a year-end rush.

Hopefully managerial time can be more effectively used and negative vibes from valued employees in our organizations can be reduced by designing feedback loops that do not undermine morale and the line manager's credibility.

I am proud that Ong Teong Wan, one of our highly regarded graduates, has made such a clear-headed and experience-backed effort to refresh us all. This seemingly basic but important book needs to be taken seriously.

Jack G. Lewis, Ph.D.
Associate Dean,
IBEAR MBA & International MBA Outreach
Marshall School of Business
University of Southern California

PREFACE

Strategy implementation is the differentiation

I was in the meeting room of a local enterprise waiting to meet with the Chief Executive Officer. To get a feel for the company, I read the Mission and Vision Statements posted on the wall. Below these, in bold print, was a slogan-like statement:

Strategy Implementation is the Differentiation.

The CEO arrived, and after exchanging pleasantries, I asked him about the statement, which seemed like an exhortation to his staff.

He explained his approach. "We are a small player in the market," he said, "and I will not expend resources to engage in sophisticated strategy formulations. We adopt a simple strategy, which is not vastly different from what most in this business do. We all adopt more or less the same strategies. Furthermore, product and pricing differentiations diminish over time. So how do we compete, except to do the right things right and do them better?"

To illustrate this, he sketched this diagram of an iceberg on the whiteboard.

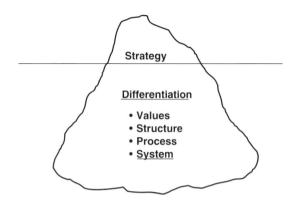

I asked him why he had underlined the last bullet point.

"A management system will hold together the other three critical success factors for our company," he explained. "Corporate values may seem to be airy-fairy public relations stuff, but if people can really see the real import of living and breathing life into these values, they will find that they actually bond people, and they are indeed the lifeblood of the organization. The value system is the glue that holds the organization together, just like a family is bonded by truly shared values. Dysfunctional teams—and organizations—lack this."

To ensure that the values can be lived and are not mere platitudes, he explained, the organization can breathe life into them "by measuring value-driven activities like rituals, ceremonies, celebrations, traditions, and inductions. These are similar to activities performed in schools and communities, and they inculcate values. Likewise, business policies and procedures in business functions do ensure adherence to company values."

He stressed, however, that it is more important to "measure and appraise people against these values, and recognize and reward people for making these values a part of their working lives in the organization. Most, if not all, of the world's highly regarded companies are all values-strong and values-driven."

Intrigued by this perspective, I suggested that as well as looking at the business tangibles and numbers to predict outcomes stock analysts in the future would also be examining intangibles such as organizational values.

He agreed: "If we are fortunate enough to grow, either organically or by acquisition, we must have the same values mindset to provide impact to our brand. We can implant our organization structure. We can replicate our product/service delivery processes. We can export our management system. But without a set of values to show employees why we are doing things in a certain way—our way—these will merely be mechanical actions without passion or commitment. We need an organization with a character of its own to differentiate."

While I agreed with him, I pointed out that we cannot ignore how the organization is structured, how the product/service delivery process is executed operationally, or the need for a uniform integrated management system to provide the infrastructure to hold regional and global entities together.

He fully agreed: "That is part of breathing life into the values we hold dear. Most operational and interface problems that retard competitiveness are not reflected in organization charts. These charts look neat and logical. Unfortunately, however, energy-dissipating and emotionally draining role conflicts seldom reach top management levels, especially when matrix organization structures become necessary as a company becomes regional or global. Functional overlaps arise, authority levels get blurred, and accountabilities are neglected or avoided, resulting in loss of productivity. Organizations become less efficient, less effective, and less competitive."

I observed: "So you have to anticipate and resolve role conflicts by clarifying roles and assigning accountabilities."

He agreed: "Very much so. I might add that accountabilities must be specific, measurable and results-focused. In fact, we should require these to be written into job descriptions, which often cover only functional descriptions of duties and leave accountabilities as general expectations."

Again, I was intrigued and asked him to tell me more about the product/service delivery process.

"Most of us strive to compile our operational procedures to meet ISO certification requirements. We draw up flow-charts and procedures, but we do not pay much attention to detailing the specific results required from each step in the processes. But if only we could detail these results, members in the product/service delivery process would feel that they are managing a business within a business, and the next person in the delivery process is the internal or, ultimately, the external customer. Theoretically, we can outsource every step in the delivery process.''

From his explanation it was clear that a system, such as a management system, provides the linkages to the value system, the inter-functional working relationships in the organization, and the product/service delivery process. ''If all these are done according to specifications, to keep the system intact and functional, then a company will be that much stronger and more resilient in the face of competition,'' I observed.

He agreed: ''When all the values, structures, processes and systems are in place, we would have provided the environment for people to work as a team, making teambuilding retreats a refresher rather than a corrective action. You see, most people will behave according to the environment that management creates. Senior management can inculcate and establish these values, structures, processes and systems but the line manager makes them work.''

I had come visiting as a consultant. I left that meeting feeling inspired.

Ong Teong Wan
www.managementwisetraining.com

Introduction

Selecting a management system to enhance productivity

A system is an operating entity that links and integrates elements, parts, structures, processes and sub-systems into a functioning whole.

For the CEO of the local enterprise mentioned in the Preface, a management system was necessary for his organization to differentiate itself, compete better and grow faster.

However, not all management systems ensure functionality. Some can be more dysfunctional than effective and can induce unproductive behavior in the workplace. This can be the result of system weaknesses, poor implementation or a combination of the two. Therefore, choosing the appropriate management system to get work done through and with people to achieve results is an important management undertaking.

The following discourse with a training manager on her organization's training needs led to a review of a common management system, the organization's performance-appraisal system.

Ascertaining Training Needs for a Management System

I was working as an external consultant with a large organization, Resu Co., whose Training Manager, Tracy Chan, was briefing me on the organization's training needs and programs for the ensuing year. Her assessment included the need for line managers and supervisors to be better trained on how to conduct performance-appraisal interviews and make appropriate ratings.

"We have conducted several training sessions which were well rated," Tracy explained, "but many of those who have been trained still experience difficulty each year." To illustrate the difficulties, she produced the following list highlighted by line managers:

Difficulties with making appraisal ratings using the current system

- No matter how well defined, the descriptors for the appraisal ratings are subject to interpretation (or misinterpretation) by appraiser and appraisee alike.

- Some appraisers are more lenient, and some have high standards and strict expectations. This affects staff morale, as people sometimes compare their appraisal ratings with one another, even though these are meant to be private and confidential.

- Some appraisal factors are traits rather than performance. They should be used for assessing potential for development, rather than for rewarding contributions to the previous year's results. Considering them together distorts the actual performance results of the past year.

- Appraisal of "Job Knowledge" depends on the appraiser's wealth of knowledge or specialization. If an appraiser is appraising someone whose field of specialization is not similar to the appraiser's, naturally by comparison, the specialist job holder will get a higher rating. On the other hand, if an appraiser is more knowledgeable than the appraisee, the appraisee may not get a high rating.

- "Job Knowledge" and "Attitude" contribute to a person's performance and are means to an end, not ends in themselves. They are best assessed separately for development purposes, rather than for rewarding for the previous year's contributions.

- Factors like "Resourcefulness" and "Teamwork" are difficult to rate even though definitions are given.

- Ratings tend to take into account performance based on recall. If an appraiser is transferred to manage a new department during the year, the appraisee's performance prior to the change may not be taken into account, or it could be forgotten or lost.

- There are also the proverbial "recency effect" (when the appraiser remembers only recent events) and the "halo effect" (when one outstanding event overshadows other work done) to consider.

Difficulties in conducting year-end appraisal discussions using the current system

- In most appraisal discussions, both the appraiser and the appraisee end up trying to recall events and incidents to justify or disagree with a rating on a factor.

- Assertive subordinates, whose perceptions about their own performance may be different from the appraiser's, often put the appraiser on the defensive. By the same token, a domineering appraiser can also put the appraisee on the defensive.

- There is nothing much to discuss if the appraisee is reticent or the appraiser is inarticulate, particularly with people whose first language is not English.

- With tense and confrontational situations, training on how to conduct interviews has limited effectiveness.

- An appraiser's overall rating is sometimes adjusted by a counter-signing superior, whose appraisal is sometimes more impressionistic or based on hearsay, rather than on first-hand knowledge. This renders the appraiser's original ratings ineffectual and meaningless.

I reassured Tracy that the line managers were not alone in facing these difficulties if their appraisal system used the behavior-anchored rating scales (BARS). While training in appraisal interviewing skills may alleviate some of the difficulties, it may not eliminate them if it is a systemic weakness. I then asked to look at the company's appraisal form, as shown in Table A. This utilized a behavior-anchored rating scale (BARS) system.

I could see that all the descriptors were intentions, rather than specific, measurable results. Measurability enables the appraiser to

TABLE A. EMPLOYEE APPRAISAL FORM USING A BARS SYSTEM

Appraisal Rating	Wt	Description	Appraisal Rating					Wt Score
			5	4	3	2	1	
Quantity of Work	4	Consistently high output Varying high output Does work normally expected Works less than normally expected Low output						
Quality of Work	5	Very accurate and thorough Exceeds expectations for accuracy and thoroughness Meets expectations for accuracy and thoroughness Below expectations for accuracy and thoroughness Inaccurate and incomplete						
Resourcefulness	4	Exceptionally enterprising—goes beyond routine work Seeks and accepts responsibility Occasionally goes beyond job responsibilities Seldom assumes greater responsibility Does routine job with little original thought and shuns responsibility						

	Wt	
Job Knowledge	3	In-depth knowledge of all aspects of job
		Good working knowledge of job details and tries to acquire more
		Adequate knowledge for normal requirements
		Has limited knowledge. Needs to improve
		Knowledge inadequate and makes little effort to learn more
Teamwork	5	Maintains excellent relations with peers and goes out of the way to assist all the time
		Good team worker. Assists without being asked
		Works and cooperates reasonably well with most
		Generally works well with people but not always cooperative
		Uncooperative and helps reluctantly when asked

Weighting (Wt)

4 to 5 Very Important

2 to 3 Quite Important

0 to 1 Less Important

Performance Categories (Weighted Score)

A – Outstanding Performer	Above 100
B – Excellent Performer	80 to 100
C – Good Performer	60 to 79
D – Satisfactory Performer	40 to 59
E – Poor Performer	Below 40

give an unequivocal "yes" or "no" as to whether the appraisee has or has not achieved the intention as written.

I am not saying that appraisers cannot have a good intuitive feel, perhaps based on long years of experience and observation, to make a valid judgment of someone's behavior. However, validity and reliability are two key considerations in measurement. Thus, when we rely on line managers with varying experiences and an intuitive feel of things to evaluate performance, this usually results in the difficulties listed above.

But the company's difficulties in this regard were by no means limited to Tracy's list and she recounted for me the experience of the Recruitment Manager who, she said, was upset that he had missed half a month's bonus by just one weighted average point in the performance-appraisal rating.

It transpired that the Recruitment Manager was rated a Good Performer with a weighted score of 79, just missing the Excellent Performer rating by one point. He was rated four in all factors except for Teamwork, for which he was rated three.

He believed that he was a good team worker. He attended all departmental meetings, contributed suggestions, and even allowed the unused part of his expense budget to be used by others.

He was told that he should have interacted and lunched more frequently with his peers, as this was considered part of team spirit. He explained that his interviewing schedules sometimes did not permit him to have leisurely lunches; in fact, he sometimes had to skip lunch altogether. The fact that he often ate alone and hurriedly was seen as him not being with the group.

However, since his superior had been most helpful and encouraging in all other respects, the Recruitment Manager did not argue with him, even though he believed that he deserved an excellent rating. That solitary point about not lunching and interacting with others probably cost him his bonus.

Logically, if there is a range, there must be a cut-off point. But missing out on a bonus by a single point can be very difficult to accept emotionally. There also seems to be arbitrariness about what score to award based on the descriptors. Why is this a three and not a four? The Recruitment Manager probably gave good reasons why he should be awarded a four, just as the supervisor could justify awarding a three, based on his interpretation of teamwork.

DISTRIBUTION OF RATINGS WITH CONVENTIONAL APPRAISAL SYSTEM

So the perceived subjectivity of evaluation or appraisal every year often culminates in appraisees becoming cynical and appraisers finding it an annual chore. When this happens, the purpose of a performance appraisal loses its significance.

There is another phenomenon which many HR managers and directors are aware of. This happens when the HR department collates all the appraisal-rating returns and looks at the distribution of ratings, across the organization, by division, or by department. There are some typical distributions of ratings.

The skewed distribution shown in Figure A is a common phenomenon. With conventional BARS-based appraisal systems, where ratings are discussed with appraisees in "open appraisals," there is a tendency for raters to skew their ratings to the positive. When asked about this, most appraisers will say that their people are good, and that's why most of them have good ratings. If bonuses and increments were to be based on the generous ratings as given, then wage costs would escalate without commensurate increases in productivity.

The real reason behind the skew is that appraisers will be put on the defensive when ratings are based on behavior and personality

FIGURE A. SKEWED DISTRIBUTION OF RATINGS—OPEN APPRAISAL

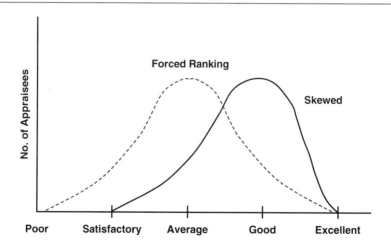

traits. They will have to explain to their appraisees, often not convincingly, their unfavorable ratings.

For example, if you rate someone "satisfactory" or "poor" on resourcefulness or teamwork, you will have to justify the rating with examples. The appraisee may come up with examples why he should be rated better. So it is one person's interpretation versus another's. Favorable ratings will be more acceptable to the appraisee, and most (but not all) appraisers will tend to shy away from unfavorable ratings to avoid arguments. They may even be doing so with the idea that this will motivate their subordinates.

Given the skewed ratings, most organizations have to moderate the returns, requiring a forced ranking into a normal or "bell-shaped" distribution. This means using a statistical device to correct inconsistencies of judgment. Employees, however, see this as setting a quota for ratings, thus causing them to perceive the appraisal ratings by individual appraisers as irrelevant.

When asked for an explanation by a disappointed appraisee, appraisers often use the forced-ranking results to relieve themselves of the responsibility for an unfavorable assessment. Appraisees are then left to wonder why they bothered going through the process in the first place if those who are most familiar with their work can be overruled in this way by a moderation committee.

Another BARS-based rating distribution (see Figure B) has appraisals in the form of confidential reports or closed appraisals. Here, countersigning superiors usually endorse or approve the ratings to provide a form of check and balance to the ratings. In such situations, there is a tendency to bunch ratings around *average*. This is because very unfavorable ratings would have to be discussed with the appraisee, and very favorable ratings would have to be justified to the countersigning superior, especially if the latter is likely to think otherwise.

Such bunched ratings will result in good contributors not feeling recognized and rewarded; consequently, talent may be lost.

Weak performers, on the other hand, will not see a need to improve, especially if most people are getting about the same rating and reward for doing the minimum. They will not go beyond their normal routine, because there is no great incentive to improve their performance.

FIGURE B. BUNCHED DISTRIBUTION OF RATINGS—CLOSED APPRAISAL

Companies that use this conventional method will find that the issues and contention still persist, no matter how many times they revise the forms and redefine the factors or behavioral descriptions. More training in performance-appraisal interviewing skills simply treats the symptom rather than the cause of the tensions over behavior/personality-based appraisal systems.

MULTI-RATER OR 360-DEGREE APPRAISAL SYSTEM

To change the perception of individual bias that accompanies the BARS system, some organizations supplement this with the 360-degree appraisal system. This involves more appraisers who have work contact with the performer, but they use more or less the same behavioral and traits factors.

Although appealing in concept, in practice the 360-degree appraisal system does not seem suited for a pay-for-performance reward system. Apart from the logistics involved, in some organizations the 360-degree appraisal system has turned out to be an annual popularity or opinion poll. There is also a tendency for ratings to skew towards the favorable, because those who have to appraise or provide feedback are usually conscious of the impact of their appraisal on the appraisee's bonus or increment.

Also, supervising or line managers may tend to minimize their responsibility in evaluating and giving feedback on their subordinates' performance, since others also have a part to play in deciding performance levels of the appraisee, regardless of the extent and intensity of inter-functional work interactions. This notion of shared responsibility may result in line managers abdicating their responsibility and authority. However, multi-rater feedback is useful for assessment and development of potential and talent.

RESULTS-BASED APPRAISAL SYSTEM

A results-based appraisal system, though not perfect, is less contentious and more valid and reliable than the systems outlined above. A results-based appraisal system is derived from the Management by Objectives (MBO) system advocated by Peter Drucker in *The Practice of Management* in the 1950s. However, Drucker advocated setting objectives, or specifying desired results, to achieve better results from an organizational and operational perspective. It was not a performance-appraisal system per se.

A results-based appraisal system allows an appraiser to evaluate performance and award appraisal ratings based on a balanced set of specific targets. Such systems use objective measures that are more specific than descriptors, thus allowing less room for divergent interpretations. In this way, people can focus on the purpose of performance appraisal, which is to achieve greater productivity. Under this system, performance appraisals are not mere annual rituals to justify pre-determined bonus awards or increments.

Table B provides a quick comparison of the common appraisal systems that may be used in the context of wage restructuring that has become necessary in light of rising operating costs that demand commensurate improvements in productivity.

RESULTS-MANAGEMENT SYSTEM

After working with several organizations on this issue, I feel we need to look at the system globally as a *results-management system*, to give a greater emphasis to results and productivity.

Table B. Performance-Appraisal Systems Compared

Features	Behavior-Anchored Rating Scales (Conventional Appraisal System)	360-Degree Appraisal (Multi-Rater Feedback)	Results-Based Appraisal System (MBO-linked)
What it is	Appraisal ratings based on desired behaviors and traits made by immediate superior, usually on a five-point rating scale	Appraisal ratings made by those who have working contact with employee Ratings made on the same behavioral factors as BARS, using a five-point rating scale	Appraisal ratings based on quantity and quality of specific results Level of difficulty and level of importance of each result area are factored in
Focus	Behavior or traits that affect performance	Feedback for personal development	Intermediate and end results desired
Role of Appraiser	Judge	One of many providing feedback	Assessing and regulating work in progress and work completed
Role of Appraisee	Understand and accept ratings	Act on feedback	Ownership of results as though appraisee was running own business
Authority to Decide Rating	Immediate superior countersigning appraisals (subject to moderation)	Usually based on majority received by a committee	Consensus between appraiser and appraisee based on results or facts
Accountability of Performer	Actions and performance	Behavioral change	End results
Acceptance of Final Rating	Depends on personality strengths of appraiser and appraisee	Varies from receptive to defensive	Normally understood and accepted, because facts are hard to argue with

(continued)

TABLE B. CONTINUED

Features	Behavior-Anchored Rating Scales	360-Degree Appraisal	Results-Based Appraisal System
	(Conventional Appraisal System)	(Multi-Rater Feedback)	(MBO-linked)
Common Pitfalls	Appraisal factors contain personality evaluations, which are more appropriate for placement purposes than for rewarding the previous year's contributions	May degenerate into annual popularity polls. Good interpersonal skills mistaken for good performance skills	Inability to convert intentions into measurable results Inability to arrive at challenging and achievable targets to improve productivity Tendency to skip periodic results reviews due to large span of control

Appraising results is just one aspect of the system for enhancing productivity, and this is the concept that line managers can understand and connect with. The other aspect is the managing of performance.

A great deal of emphasis is on achieving results through and with people, and that implies substantial management of performance, besides the measuring of performance results.

In Tracy's case, although the apparent need was to train line managers on how to conduct year-end appraisal interviews, the real need was to train line managers to implement a results-management system. The thinking underlying this is that if people are managed well, performance measurement and appraisal will be made easier. Employees will be more inclined to conduct self-appraisals to evaluate their own performance and, in the right circumstances, they will generally be harsher with themselves than you might expect.

PERFORMANCE MEASUREMENT AND WAGE RESTRUCTURING

Companies have realized that wage costs represent the bulk of their operational expenses. The lower the fixed costs associated with base salary increments, the lower their fixed overheads. High overhead costs hinder competitiveness.

Consequently, there are moves to mitigate base salary increments and focus on awarding higher variable payments for good organizational and individual performance. This is to ensure that rewards are based on tangible performance results which can vary from year to year. In this way, an employee's reward is more closely linked to his real performance and the performance of the organization.

With the conventional appraisal system, productivity cannot be measured more definitively to match increasing wage costs. One well-regarded HR director once said to me, "If there's going to be a paradigm shift in the reward system, there must be a complementary paradigm shift in the current performance appraisal system."

This shift will require establishing individual performance measures, periodically reviewing results to correct and improve

FIGURE C. NORMAL DISTRIBUTION OF RATINGS

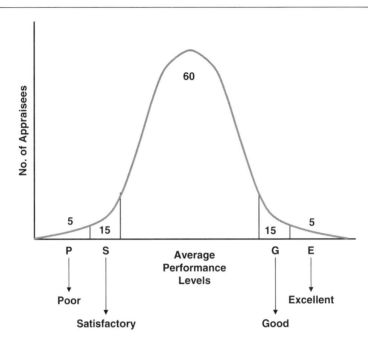

performance, evaluating final results, and emphasizing pay-for-performance to identify and retain talent. It is crucial then to provide accurate inputs to the compensation system for it to work effectively.

Ideally, the distribution of ratings should look like a normal distribution or bell-shaped curve to reflect the validity and reliability of the ratings (see Figure C).

In short, if you have a management system that incorporates individual performance measurement, performance management and performance evaluation to make individual contributors feel that they are managing a "business" within a business, then many of the usual difficulties and distortions will be reduced, if not eliminated.

It will not be an appraisal system per se, but a holistic results-management system that essentially looks at performance measurement, performance management, performance reward, talent identification and retention.

Calling it a results-management system (RMS) eradicates the notion that managing for results is doing HR's work, complying with policies and procedures and filling forms. Getting results through and with people will be seen and accepted as part of a line manager's key functions.

 Key Points to Ponder

- A strong management system is a prerequisite for effective people performance.
- A results-management system can reduce many of the difficulties and confusions associated with conventional, behavior-based appraisal systems.
- It is more cost-effective to focus training on the overall real needs of a system than on single-item apparent needs.
- An effective measurement system can help an organization to achieve wage cost-effectiveness by differentiating between good performers and weak performers so as to compensate them accordingly and retain talent.

CHAPTER ONE

OVERVIEW: THE RESULTS-MANAGEMENT SYSTEM

Achieving results through and with people

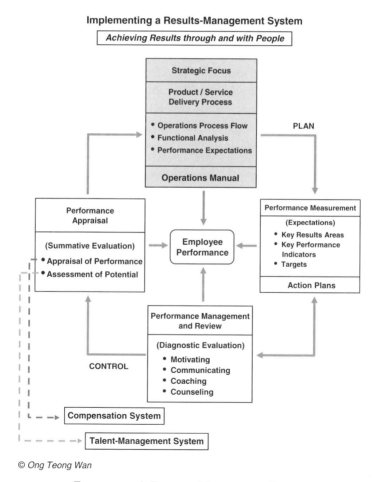

© Ong Teong Wan

FIGURE 1.1. A RESULTS-MANAGEMENT SYSTEM

THE TONE FROM THE TOP

In my experience of working with organizations over 25 years, the organizations that derived benefits from training were the ones that regarded training as an investment rather than as a cost. Regarding training as an investment means commitment to a cause. Regarding it as a cost is only involvement in an activity.

Training as an organizational intervention will not derive its full value if not applied, implemented, and practiced to the extent that it is part of the organizational culture.

Training to implement a system, process, structure, or value system across the entire organization will ensure that it becomes part of the organizational culture. It has greater value than training in discrete skills or topics. Approving budgets for training will create a climate for learning, but it does not guarantee that what is learned will become part of the organizational culture.

We are all creatures of habit—in thought and action. We take the same route to work; should there be a traffic jam, we accept it either patiently or with displeasure. Most of the time, unless there is a dire necessity to be on time, we will not make a serious effort to find an alternative route or an alternative means to get to work on time.

The same goes with identifying training needs and developing training plans.

However, we need to ask this question: Is training an end in itself, or is it a means to an end? For business organizations, it surely must be a means to an end. The end we are after is organizational effectiveness, and one of the tools to achieve this is to have a management system for line managers to use, to perform their job of getting results through and with people. That being the case, it would be best to train people to implement a management system to improve productivity or results.

This is made more pressing by the fact that wages are increasing and there should be a commensurate improvement in productivity for the organization's long-term health.

Nothing encourages a training consultant more than having the top management of an organization willing to sit in at a presentation to introduce a management system. In this, they are setting the tone from the top. At such meetings I have used the chart shown in Figure 1.1 to illustrate the workings of a results-management system.

The system has the following components:

1. *Strategic Focus for the Year:* To predetermine the near-term course of action and direct all business processes and functional activities to the collective priority of the organization for the year as a managerial planning function. Expected organizational key results areas are also made known and disseminated.

2. *Performance Measurement:* To establish performance measures to monitor and assess results for work in progress and work completed as a managerial control function. To measure what to maintain or improve in value-added functional services and activities, as well as to recognize contributions daily and periodically by individual employees.

3. *Performance Management and Review:* To impel line and support functions to take effective action as a managerial leadership function. To enable performers to achieve or exceed the functional value-added services expected of them and diagnose performance problems daily or during periodic reviews.

4. *Performance Appraisal:* To make a summative evaluation of the actual functional value-added services provided by individual employees to support the organization's vision, mission, and business objectives for the year.

5. *Compensation System:* To ensure paying for performance, paying for the job and paying market rates so as to attract and retain willing, skilled, and knowledgeable employees.

6. *Talent-Management System:* To assess potential and identify, develop, and retain talent for the long-term viability of the organization.

Ideally, all systems should be working well to ensure organizational health and effectiveness. Only then can the company's human resources be better utilized for greater productivity.

Organizational health can be likened to a person's well-being, which is dependent on whether the digestive, respiratory, reproductive, circulation, and nervous systems, separately and conjointly, are functioning well.

A results-management system, if properly implemented, will do the following:

- Encourage all employees to regard themselves as running a business within a business
- Measure their individual value-added services
- Encourage performers to appraise the extent of their individual contributions
- Motivate performers to try to do better each year
- Reward performance
- Manage talent for the long term

If every employee regards the functional responsibilities for which he was engaged as being "outsourced" to him, the notion of running a business within a business can be understood better.

Strategic Focus for the Year

A company's *strategic focus* derives from its strategic planning system.

Annually, organizations typically decide what they want to focus on prior to budgeting, which is allocating resources to meet profit targets.

An organization might focus on growing the business, increasing profits, increasing market share, containing costs, improving customer relations, strengthening corporate values, and other actions and initiatives to take the company forward. Having decided on that, all divisions and departments will implement the initiatives through the product/service-delivery system and the results-management system.

The various functional divisions and departments will set their targets to support the focus for the year. For example, if the focus is to reduce operating costs by 10 percent for the year, all divisions and departments will see where most of their operating costs are, identify the critical few, and set a target accordingly to reduce the operating cost.

Sales could look at advertising, entertainment or transportation costs, while Production could look at the costs of raw materials, overtime, inventory, or warehousing.

HR could look at medical, recruitment, and uniform costs, and Finance could look at documentation and legal costs, and so on.

PERFORMANCE MEASUREMENT

Performance measurement is the target-setting part of the results-management system. Before targets are set, the needs areas for which key results areas are identified and targets are set by divisions, departments, and individuals have to be reviewed and established.

These areas could involve targets to capture **opportunities**, such as acquiring new office space when rentals are down, cornering the market with a new product or service or maximizing business incentives provided by the government or other opportunities provided by the prevailing economic environment.

For **deficiency needs**, attention may have to be paid to some core functions that might not have achieved the desired results or performance standards for the previous year. These situations must be corrected by, for example, improving yields, reducing employee turnover, reducing receivables, or increasing market share.

There could be some ongoing targets or standards—such as zero defects or zero accidents—that need to be **maintained**. All these could be in addition to **special assignment needs** or directives from the top, such as reducing operating costs that have to be cascaded down to the individual employee.

PERFORMANCE MANAGEMENT AND REVIEW

This is truly the bedrock of the results-management system and not the performance-measurement system that most people will conclude it to be. In fact, this is the most overlooked aspect of a results-management system, as many are more preoccupied with key performance indicators than with how to enable employees to achieve them.

It is not uncommon to hear that organizations embarking on a results-based appraisal system will set targets at the beginning of the year, and scramble to assemble data at the end of the year with which to appraise.

Appraiser and appraisee then get into conflicting situations without adequate supporting data. Both parties then become discouraged with a system that is supposed to be more objective and less contentious than the conventional behavior-anchored rating scales.

If performance management was considered a necessary aspect of such a system and reviews were conducted, actual results updated, and trouble-shooting done, there would be fewer or no surprises at year end. The performer could even do a self-appraisal of results achieved against results expected.

Competencies for performance management and review are commonly referred to as "soft skills" or "interpersonal relations skills." These include skills on listening, handling differences of opinion, positive and constructive feedback, as well as performance coaching and counseling.

These skills make up the *performance management and review* part of the system. This is the part where the manager really earns his keep by developing an open and trusting working relationship with subordinates.

This is the art of managing for commitment and not for compliance with targets. There must be a balance between the results desired and the motivation to achieve them.

Setting targets to specify desired results is part of the planning and control function of management. This involves assessing and regulating work in progress or work completed and results achieved against plan. It is a logical, left-brain activity.

However, if it were just a matter of an employee meeting or not meeting targets and being evaluated accordingly, it would really only be managing for compliance with targets. With such a narrow orientation, most ordinary mortals will try to set conservative targets so that they will not fail. If you raise the bar, people become apprehensive and try to resist. They will be bargaining at target-setting time.

Indeed, this is one of the reasons why MBO systems in some organizations are not as successful as they should be. Even though the concept makes a lot of sense, it requires emotional engagement as well. This is why time should be allocated for performance-management training, to support the results-management system.

PERFORMANCE APPRAISAL

A typical management controlling process starts with establishing performance measures, taking measurements of results attained to date, evaluating the actual results achieved against expected results (which is also known as "appraising") and then taking whatever corrective follow-up action is necessary.

During performance reviews, a line manager reviews work in progress or work completed. If targets are not met, or if they are exceeded in the interim, the manager and subordinate sit down and try to ascertain the cause of the negative or positive variance against targets set. This is a diagnostic activity—finding out the real cause of a discrepancy then taking corrective or remedial action so that the desired results are achieved at year end.

At the end of the year, when the line manager and direct report take stock of the overall results for the year, it is a summation of everything. It is like a year-end examination in school. The performance-management reviews are like daily, weekly, or term tests and assessments that provide feedback in the school system. The teacher then provides individual guidance, tuition, or coaching or counseling, as necessary.

In year-end appraising, managers not only appraise performance on results achieved, but they also assess potential based on behaviors and attributes shown in the pursuit of the results expected. The results from these are then fed into the compensation system, which recognizes performance and team membership with bonuses and increments.

The data on the strengths and weaknesses of the performer is also fed into the talent-management system, which looks at career-development directions for the individual and succession planning for the organization's long-term growth.

COMPENSATION SYSTEM

Within the results-management system, the *compensation system* is a necessary complement to performance appraisal.

The pay-for-performance aspect of the compensation system is linked to the appraisal ratings in the summative evaluation. It recognizes productivity and provides positive or negative consequences for performance, so as to make performance matter.

Many organizations are now restructuring their compensation systems to mitigate rising wage costs by according lower annual increments to the base pay and have a large variable bonus component based on results achieved for the year.

It is recognized that base-pay increments even with lower percentages, when compounded over the years, can escalate fixed wage costs. The basis for such increments is more to reflect cost-of-living increases. Some organizations also take into account competency development or adherence to corporate values to provide a basis for granting a higher increment beyond the normal cost-of-living increase.

Results-based variable bonuses depend on an effective results-management system to be effective motivators to productive employees.

TALENT-MANAGEMENT SYSTEM

If the results-management system only culminates with the compensation system, it will be incomplete. The system is meant to achieve results currently and also for the future. Talent needs to be identified and developed to ensure the organization continues to be productive to achieve expected results over the long term.

The *talent-management system* is linked to the assessment of potential within the results-management system and it helps the organization to identify, nurture, and retain talent to ensure its continued viability.

Talent management is harnessing intellectual capital for the organization's long-term growth and survival. It is not an exact science, as assessing human ability on acquired know-how and know-why is also an art, notwithstanding the many profiling instruments available to the line manager to use in addition to on-the-job assessment of potential.

Key Points to Ponder

- Training to implement a structure, process or system provides the organizational climate and culture to re-inforce things learned.

- The components of a results-management system are: Strategic Focus for the year; Establishing Performance Measures; Managing and Reviewing Performance with motivation, communication, coaching and counseling; Appraising Performance; Assessing Potential; Recognizing and Rewarding Performance; and Talent Management for the future.

- A results-management system is not all about results and measurement. Performance management is the key.

- All parts and sub-systems of a management system need to work well to enable the whole system to function well.

- All parts of a management system are interlinked and mutually supportive.

CHAPTER TWO

PERFORMANCE MEASUREMENT

Anything measured gets done. Anything measured gets improved

Implementing a Results-Management System

Achieving Results through and with People

Strategic Focus

Product / Service Delivery Process

- Operations Process Flow
- Functional Analysis
- Performance Expectations

Operations Manual

PLAN

Performance Appraisal

(Summative Evaluation)
- Appraisal of Performance
- Assessment of Potential

Employee Performance

Performance Measurement

(Expectations)
- Key Results Areas
- Key Performance Indicators
- Targets

Action Plans

Performance Management and Review

(Diagnostic Evaluation)
- Motivating
- Communicating
- Coaching
- Counseling

CONTROL

Compensation System

Talent-Management System

© Ong Teong Wan

At Resu Co., I commenced the training session on establishing individual performance measures by writing on the flipchart the following rallying call by proponents of Total Quality Management. This was familiar to all the divisional directors and departmental managers assembled in the seminar room.

Anything Measured Gets Done.
Anything Measured Gets Improved.

I often used to wonder whether anything measured got things done and improved automatically, without external impetus. It probably does for mountaineers and adventurers who have the need for self-fulfillment, but for ordinary mortals like us? The only occasion I was prompted to do something when measured was when the doctor told me that my cholesterol level was too high and I had to watch my diet. I did. I stayed off fatty foods, ate more fruits and vegetables and walked more often. My family supportively abided by the new emphasis in our daily diet. There was concerted commitment from everyone.

I asked the gathering what they thought of the two statements. Were they realistic, idealistic or self-fulfilling?

Henry volunteered the following: "For an organization to get the results it desires, I guess there has to be concerted vested interest in the measures and the results, and what they really mean to everyone in the organization. There has to be commitment to the results desired. Just establishing measures of performance may not automatically get things done or improved. We need the passion and the commitment to achieve a broader purpose with the specific measures as guideposts so as not to lose direction."

This proved to be very helpful in setting the tone for the ensuing discussion.

MEASUREMENT TERMS

I listed two groups of words related to measurement on the whiteboard and asked the participants for the difference between the two.

Group A	Group B
goals	targets
aims	specific objectives
purposes	
general objectives	
key results areas	
key performance indicators	

The participants volunteered various interpretations and concluded that the words in Group A connoted general directions, intangibles, intentions, and expectations. The words in Group B meant specific outcomes or results desired.

Most of the time, people are more comfortable stating generalities ("I would like to be successful one day") than being specific ("I want to have $2 million cash by the time I'm 50"). Consequently, most targets are couched more in terms of intentions or expectations, rather than specific results desired. Being specific gives the impetus to achievement whereas an intention could remain just a desire or a wish.

HOW WE NORMALLY SET TARGETS

The participants were asked to write down how they normally set targets in their respective areas of work. The results they came up with included the following:

Sales: To increase top-line sales by 15 percent over last year.

Production: To meet the production schedule for the year.

HR: To fill all vacancies by agreed dates, with all new recruits accepted by requesting line managers.

Facilities: To complete office renovation by 2Q of the following year.

Finance and Accounting: To complete all required monthly reports by their due dates.

Engineering: To reduce unscheduled downtime from 25 percent to 20 percent by March.

IT: To ensure that computer downtime is limited to no more than 15 minutes for counter staff and an hour for office staff.

Both Sales and Production said that they had set their respective targets well because they met the SMART criteria (that is, of being **s**pecific, **m**easurable, **a**chievable, **r**elevant and **t**ime-based).

Targets are usually considered difficult to set for support groups, as not all their work is deemed quantifiable. Nevertheless, every functional group, be it a revenue or a cost center, has a contribution to make to the organization. However, the fact is that we are not used to establishing performance measures for the less-tangible and indirect contributions for them to be seen as partners to the enterprise, and this is something that needs to be addressed.

It is a common misconception that meeting the SMART criteria is all there is to proper measurement. Using these criteria, which are actually a checklist, requires that targets are set according to specifications. However, we need to look beyond meeting the SMART criteria for setting targets or establishing performance measures.

SMART says that targets must be specific, measurable, achievable, relevant and time-based. Though I have no quarrel with the specifications, they are not helpful in determining relevant key results areas. A checklist is not necessarily a thinking process.

Targets are specific results expected and are closely related to the needs, intentions or expectations of the organization's internal or external customers, as well as the aspirations of the one setting the targets.

For example, the intention to increase the organization's top-line sales revenue will contribute tangibly to its gross revenue. But what about collections? What about the quality of the product or the service level provided? What about the cost incurred in selling and collecting? Is the customer's overall satisfaction great enough for him to want to continue to do business with you or refer other businesses to you?

Assuming the top-line sales target is met or exceeded, but the collections are less than 50 percent on due dates, does that constitute a good sales performance?

Did the goods or services sold meet customer requirements, or were there returned goods? Were re-dos or re-designs needed? What expenses were incurred to achieve the sales revenue?

To be in the business for the long haul, the human or emotional aspect of meeting the target has to be taken into account too. If the relationship with the customer is good, beyond pricing and meeting specifications, the organization can be better assured of continuing business and referrals. With this in mind, organizations that pay sales commissions based on sales revenue alone would be well-advised to review their system. As Sally put it: "Professionalism in sales is not just achieving the top-line revenue."

BALANCING EFFICIENCY MEASURES WITH EFFECTIVENESS MEASURES

This line of thinking prompted Paul to observe that in the Production area, too, their concerns were not limited to volume and timing: "We also have to worry about yield and meeting quality specifications. We must also consider unit costs, and have to ensure that in achieving our targets, our production operators are not so overworked that they have to take medical leave or get into accidents through tiredness. If they are so stressed that they resign, our future production schedules and production yield will not be met. We have to look after the customer well; but we also have to look after our own people well."

This opened the way for broadening the discussion to setting targets for the support groups. In recruitment, for example, this might require that the department adopt a position where it looks on itself as an outsourced recruitment agency engaged to recruit for the company. In doing so, it will focus more closely on what the line managers as internal clients require. As Ravi, the Recruitment Manager, put it in the course of our discussions, this would entail meeting "a broad set of expectations from our internal clients: that all vacancies be filled as soon as they become available; that all the applicants we shortlist meet the job specifications given to us; that we recruit as cost-effectively as possible and within salary grades; and that we don't recruit people who are likely to quit before they complete their probation."

This insight into the need for a balanced set of measures was reflected in the comments from the other support departments. Felix, from Facilities Management, spoke not simply of renovating the office within budget and by target date, but in such a way that there should be no need for further re-wiring, re-cabling, or touch-ups after handover and employees would be delighted with the new office. Frank said that his monthly financial reports would be "useful, readable, and user-friendly" and produced "without engaging temps or incurring overtime expenses." Above all, he guaranteed that they would be free from the errors that had made previous offerings "of little or no value to end-users."

In my experience, in organizations where targets are perceived to be something of a carrot-and-stick tool, the training sessions are muted and participants guarded and inhibited. However, it need not be like this, as the enthusiasm generated by the participants in this session clearly showed. Having participants from all areas of the business discuss and clearly articulate their expectations of each other in this way can sharpen the focus of each on how they can contribute by way of internal service to the overall health of the organization. In the Engineering and IT areas, for example, such considerations might include not only reducing machine/computer downtime and the attendant repair and maintenance costs, but also ensure that production's product quality is not compromised. Important, too, is the attitude that the various technicians might take to requests for assistance from the machine operators when machines are down. Including the reactions of the end-users to the maintenance team's support service can be another of those intangibles that can be so important. Good working relationships affect teamwork and productivity.

Two components are important in setting balanced targets for individual performance: efficiency and effectiveness.

To be able to deliver a quantity of product or service within a stipulated timeframe is being efficient. However, managers need to look at the quality of the service or product, the cost of achieving quantity and time targets, as well as the human reaction or impact associated with the achievement of the other expected results. This could be considered the effectiveness of the target. When we set targets, we need to establish a balance between being efficient and being effective, the characteristics of which are set out in Table 2.1 below.

TABLE 2.1. BALANCING EFFICIENCY WITH EFFECTIVENESS

Efficiency	Effectiveness
quantity	quality
time	cost
	human reaction/impact

The Process of Establishing Performance Measures

Once we have a thinking process to establish performance measures, we can actually establish these measures and set targets for any field of human endeavor.

For example, when we looked at the Sales group's presentation earlier, we concluded that achieving a particular sales revenue within a certain timeframe was not enough to constitute a good sales performance, which also had to incorporate meeting customer expectations and being cost-effective in making the sale. This involves watching the expenses incurred in making the sale (such as entertainment and travel expenses), not forgetting customer satisfaction and fostering sound human relationships to ensure a long-term business relationship.

Key Results Areas

In essence, we are translating our intentions or customer expectations into what are called **key results areas**, or the important types of results that are of value to the organization or the customer.

The generic key results areas are quantity, time, quality, cost and human reaction or human impact. It is critical that we ask ourselves the following question: What are the key results areas to consider when we try to define good performance in a particular activity?

To let the managers gain a deeper insight into the process of establishing performance measures, all participants were asked to work on salary administration, which was outside of their usual area of expertise and which many thought of as being difficult to measure.

Beatrice, the Compensation and Benefits Manager, was on hand to answer any queries they had about key issues involved in salary administration. She explained that salary administration comprised job evaluations to ensure internal equity among jobs, salary surveys to assess prevalent market rates for their jobs, and paying for performance or contributions to the organization's business.

The managers then jotted down what they thought were key results areas to achieve in a good salary survey. Their suggestions were as follows:

Efficiency

Number of participating companies

Completion date

Effectiveness

Type of participating companies

Extent of confidential data shared

Cost of project

Acceptance of survey data

For a survey to be of any value it must be completed in time for participants and users of the survey data to do their salary planning. So timing is a key result area.

The number and types of companies participating in the survey are also crucial. Information on how many companies would need to be targeted to yield sufficient data to make the survey valid and reliable could be supplied by the HR department. So this is another key result area.

We then explored the costs involved and Henry was able to give us the benefit of his experience. "If we do it ourselves, it will be our time cost," he said. "If we outsource it, then the fees payable to the survey organization will be the actual direct cost." All agreed that cost was another key result area.

Henry then went on to give an HR perspective on what makes for a high-quality survey. "For it to be of any real use to us, all the participating companies must be from within the same industry, and thus likely to compete for talent with us, and be of a comparable type and size."

Here, Frank chipped in with the view that the extent to which the data shared among participating companies is confidential also needs to be clarified. "The identities specific to the data can be kept confidential, but there should not be any withholding of important data," he emphasized. "If most of the responses indicate 'highly sensitive and confidential, cannot be released,' then the quality is suspect. Truthfulness, completeness, and accuracy are important considerations in a salary survey among participating companies."

Employees, whose salaries are based on the results of such surveys, have to be able to trust the data, even if they may not agree with the proposed pay adjustments based on the data. They need to know that the survey can be used as a rational and objective basis to formulate salary plans and that the data has not been cooked up by the company to justify predetermined salary adjustments.

This key result area, which I would call "human reaction" or "impact on people," completes what I would call an individual balanced scorecard, to borrow current terminology.

Drawing out such information from senior personnel and seeing their growing awareness of the importance of such steps makes it more likely that this performance-measurement process percolates through the entire organization. Step 1 in the process is to state intentions or expectations. Step 2 is to list the key results areas. Having identified the areas of value pertinent to the intentions and expectations, Step 3 would logically be to establish ways of measuring results areas; that is, key performance indicators (KPI).

Key Performance Indicators

A KPI is a unit or type of measure. For example, the key results areas for an economy are economic growth, inflation, and employment levels. The KPIs are expressed in gross domestic product or gross national product, inflation rates, and employment rates. A key result area for weather is temperature and the KPI is either in degrees Celsius or Fahrenheit. For rainfall we have indicators in millimeters, centimeters, or inches. For wind speed we have the Beaufort scale. For health, the common key results areas are cholesterol level, blood pressure, and sugar level. The medical profession has created KPIs to measure cholesterol level (total, high density/low density) in mg/dL, blood pressure (systolic/ diastolic) in mmHg, and sugar (glucose) level in mg/dL, developing their special units of measure.

Most of the KPIs we use are absolute numbers, ratios, percentages, or points. Special KPIs are developed by professionals or specialists within their particular fields.

I then gave the participants an example of a land transport authority that had developed the key results areas and KPIs to measure the efficiency and effectiveness of taxi company services in the country. Table 2.2 shows that the organization was able to identify what were quantity, time, quality (of service), cost, human impact, and human reaction.

TABLE 2.2. TAXI SERVICE LEVEL

Key Results Areas	Key Performance Indicators
Distances traveled with passengers	Average paid mileage per day per taxi
Level of taxi occupancy	Average utilization rate per taxi
Response to radio calls for taxis	Radio response rate
Safety record	Number of accidents per taxi
Passenger satisfaction	Complaints per 100 taxis

It is fairly common to hear people talking about KPIs as though they are targets: the terms are often used as if they were interchangeable, in the same way that "objectives" and "goals" have been used interchangeably in the past.

However, KPIs are units of measure. A target is a specific result to be achieved, and it implies the specification of what is meant by good or not good. To return to our health example for a moment, total cholesterol level is one key result area for measuring good health. Its KPI is total cholesterol in mg/dL. According to current medical recommendations, the desirable target is 200 mg/dL or less. Therefore, 200mg/dL is a specific result desired or a target.

As Sally was quick to observe, this is a recommended universal benchmark, a target that few will dispute. "In the case of sales and marketing," she pointed out, "there are no benchmarks. The sky's the limit."

Setting Challenging and Achievable Targets

Setting targets is easy if you are talking about giving a number to the KPI. What makes it more difficult is that the targets must be challenging and yet achievable. But this could be seen as being quite subjective: what the manager may see as challenging, the direct report may perceive to be unachievable. This goes back to what we said earlier about anything measured getting done and anything measured getting improved. Things may not be done well and improved if there is no clear understanding and willing acceptance. The understanding is the logical part and the willing acceptance is the emotional part.

In truth, we are looking for commitment to the specific results desired, and not just dispassionate compliance with the targets set. It hinges on management as an art, too, and underscores the need for regular performance reviews, communication, motivation, coaching, and counseling sessions. It involves building a trusting working relationship between superior and direct report. Performers in support functions should be made to feel that they are running a business within a business with a captive clientele, meaning the internal customers. For those serving external customers, they will have to feel that they are stakeholders in the enterprise formed to serve external customers and clients.

Ideally, we would like a situation where the direct report wants to set targets that are so challenging that they have to be moderated, such that the direct report is not too demoralized when the targets are not met. If you can create such a working environment, then you have arrived as a leader and a manager of people.

The question then arises as to how to go about arriving at targets that are motivating enough for people to commit to, rather than simply to comply with.

A challenging target is one that is higher or better than the one previously achieved. But should it be slightly higher, moderately higher, or very much higher? Achievable implies that there is a high likelihood of it being achieved. The more conservative the target, the more achievable it is; conversely, the more ambitious a target, the less achievable it is.

With highly motivated individuals and those with a strong sense of mission in life, almost anything is achievable, and they are willing to take on challenges. Ordinary folks are sometimes envious and label such people "incorrigible optimists."

For the majority, especially when their bonus and reward are tied to targets, there must be a practical way to arrive at an understanding and agreement as to what constitutes a challenging and achievable target. This is not necessarily straightforward, as Tracy observed during the training session: "If you have a kind, lenient, or popularity-seeking superior, you can set targets that are easy to achieve. If you have an ambitious, demanding, or glory-seeking superior, the targets will be tough to achieve, and these are euphemistically called 'stretched targets.'"

While her observation may be true to a certain extent, it is not always the lenient and popularity-seeking superior that will use unchallenging targets. Some managers are under the mistaken impression that rewarding more than is deserved is motivating. But this is not motivating; it's manipulating. For the more demanding managers, the glory they are seeking may be elusive if people are not truly committed to the targets set.

One useful way to at least obtain understanding and acceptance is to estimate the most pessimistic and the most optimistic results expected, and then settle on a target somewhere between the two extremes.

The extremes represent low probability of occurrence; the in-between represents the relatively higher probability of achievement. You then review whether it is achievable after an agreed period, such as at the end of the first quarter.

To a certain extent, people who set low targets are not necessarily motivated by monetary rewards alone. More than anything else, they may lack confidence. These are the people who need encouragement and support with feedback and coaching.

After listening to all of this, Sally asked, "Let's say currently I have 10 complaints per month, whether justified or not, and I set a target of five complaints, which is an ambitious target. However, my boss says that in order to compete better we should have no complaints. How do we resolve this? If he insists and I have to do it, I will only be working for compliance rather than from commitment. So what should the target be?"

This produced considerable discussion among the group, with Imran pointing out that: "Having zero complaints is not necessarily a good thing. If customers don't complain, they may be taking their business elsewhere. There will be complaints, some justified and some unjustified. Some may even be misplaced notions of customer rights. Some could be beyond the control of the performer."

Martin expanded on this: "In practice, there will always be complaints and, hopefully, compliments. One way would be to set a target where compliments exceed complaints. The percentage of compliments exceeding complaints, whatever the type, should be increasing, for you to retain your customers."

Quite naturally, the discussion ventured into other areas of business activity, with Paul pointing out that the Production area was required to meet its schedules with no accidents, which was no easy target if "machines are old and workers are not safety conscious."

Asked for their comments on what they would set as a target for accidents in these circumstances, the other participants agreed that the target of zero accidents was correct. Henry pointed out, "If we really care about our people and claim that they are our most valuable asset, as many mission statements do, we have to live the talk."

When we want results to be challenging and achievable, we are thinking about being realistic. Achieving zero accidents is being realistic, as the experience of many Japanese companies has shown. If we expect zero error rates from nursing staff who dispense medicine, or from air-traffic controllers guiding planes to land, there is no reason not to have stringent targets in other areas where personal safety is concerned.

Hence, setting challenging and achievable targets should not be done mechanically as a checking-off of items on a checklist, without insight.

Tracy, who had been listening carefully to the discussion, spoke up at this point: "I have a question. Just the other day, we were discussing the need to have perfect punctuality rate in reporting for work, in case customers called and were not attended to. Objections were raised about the impossibility of achieving this because of traffic jams, crowded buses and trains, and so on. Similarly, if a machine is old and we know it will produce defects, setting zero defects as a target is one we know we cannot achieve and the will to do it won't be there. My question, then, is: Do we then take into account causal factors for not meeting a previous target, or potential causal factors when establishing new targets for the year?"

Both the reply and the source were somewhat unexpected. Frank was quite clear that "If achieving these things is a must, then it is a result to be pursued with intensity." He elaborated further with an example from his own field: "In finance, if we cannot get an injection of cash during hard economic times, we will have to fold. We simply have to find a way of getting the cash—beg, borrow, or look for a bail-out! It is a must, and creativity is demanded."

It was intriguing to hear an analytically trained person talking about the need for creativity and I was quick to reinforce the view that if a situation demands it, then it provides the rationale for the seemingly impossible target.

Most productive and dynamic companies will set the targets, and then look for ways to achieve these results, rather than giving excuses as to why they can't be achieved. Managers may understand this, but the team members down the line may not be able to perceive things with such depth of thought. Management will see it as realistic if a business situation demands it. Direct reports, on the other hand, may see it as merely being idealistic.

The tone from the top will set the climate and the culture of the place. If top management has a steadfast belief in things, and demonstrates that belief by setting equally demanding targets for themselves to address the situation, they are more likely to be able to change the mindsets of those who work under them and convince others to commit to the seemingly impossible targets.

That is leadership—not just operational management.

Action Planning

Having set the targets, the next thing to do is to take action. For project work, action plans are common. An action plan might look like that shown in Figure 2.1.

Figure 2.1. A Typical Action Plan

Action Plan

Title:_____

Efficiency: To have _____ by: _____

Effectiveness: 1. _____   Accountability for achievement of
2. _____   Results _____
3. _____   Date Action Plan Prepared: _____

What Will Be Done (Action Step)	Est. Days	When?		By Whom? Accountability	At What Cost?		Progress Check		
		Start	Deadline		Work Hours	Dollars	Started	Finished	Status

For example, marketing people planning a promotion drive may use an action plan to co-ordinate activities involving many people to achieve the results targeted. First, they list the targets set, then they brainstorm the activities, or what has to be done to achieve the targets. They then estimate the time needed for each step, and assign a person to be accountable for the completion of that step.

For each step there is a budget if direct expenditure is needed. If not, the cost will be the work hours expended relative to the duration estimated for each action step. There is provision within the plan to review the status of achievement of each step, when the team gets together to review results achieved and action taken, at periodic intervals.

Some organizations even anticipate what could go wrong at each step. They then plan preventive actions to reduce the probability of things going wrong, and institute contingency actions in case the preventive actions do not work. Others estimate the net worth of a project by comparing the value of the overall results stated in the target, and deduct the expenses incurred in effecting each of the steps.

Action planning can be useful for regular job functions such as recruitment or training programs and the steps involved can be incorporated into the company's operations manual.

ACCOUNTABILITY FOR RESULTS

As it is with any human endeavor, in any business there will always be a cause-and-effect chain. As Eugene remarked during the training session, there are times when results in the Engineering area are dependent on other people in other areas doing their part, and he gave the following example to illustrate his point: "If Purchasing is slow in procuring the machine parts we need, and the parts can't be supplied in time, then our downtime or maintenance schedule targets won't be met." Similarly, Accounts cannot produce comprehensive reports if they don't receive timely and accurate data; or production schedules can't be met if raw materials are not supplied on time or if operator vacancies are not filled with the right type of people.

When a part of the product/service-delivery process breaks down, the rest of the process is affected. However, someone has to be accountable for the results at each stage of the process. If the customer does not get his goods on time because of a disruption in the production or delivery process, the customer is going to hold Sales accountable for its commitment to delivery date. The customer will not be interested in internal cause-and-effect problems.

All departments within an organization are part of the product/service-delivery process, as illustrated in Figure 2.2. Each position-holder in the organization therefore has an internal customer who expects specific results from the internal supplier of product or service. These expected results come under the generic key results areas of quantity, time, quality, cost, and human reaction/impact.

FIGURE 2.2.   PRODUCT/SERVICE-DELIVERY PROCESS

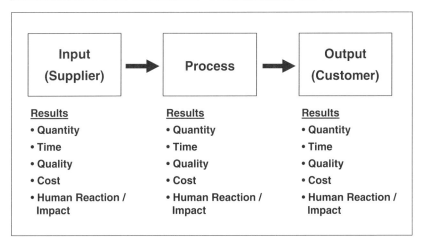

Some people ask how we can logically be accountable for disruptions in the supply chain or factors outside our direct control. The concept of delegation requires us to be accountable to the person who delegated the job to us, and this person is finally accountable to others for the results.

So, although logically we cannot be held accountable for factors beyond our control that affect our results, we are still accountable for the results expected of us. We must, therefore, anticipate and prevent potential problems that are likely to jeopardize our results. If the prevention fails then we have to take corrective or contingent action to reduce loss and the impact on overall results. If we can, we should put in place preventive measures to reduce the probability of occurrence of the likely causes for problems, so that we can be better assured of achieving the expected results.

Of course, there could be situations related to natural disasters such as earthquakes, floods, or epidemics. In such cases, managers are expected to put in place contingency plans to mitigate or reduce the severity of the impact on their results.

Every contributor to the results has to think of the "what-ifs" to work on, besides developing action plans. Planning and controlling are basic management functions.

Planning has been described as a basic management function to predetermine a future course of action which can be short term or long term. Controlling can be likened to a thermostat to assess and regulate an operation in progress or completed. Setting targets, therefore, invokes the need for planning and controlling, besides the soft skills required to manage for commitment to targets set.

The question then arises as to whether there can still be joint accountability for the same results. The answer to this is "yes." In training programs, for example, one of the key result areas may be that trainees apply what they learn. The target could be that 100 percent of participants apply what they have learned within two weeks of completing the training. The company expects returns on investment in its training efforts. So it is necessary for participants to apply what they have learned on their jobs. The problem is that when they return to their workplace, the priorities of their immediate superiors may not give them the opportunity to apply what they have learned. To ensure that their superiors support this result expected by the company, those who sent their direct reports for training should have the same key result area. In that sense, there is joint accountability.

In Sales, there could be a key result area which says sales collections are up to date. The target could be 100 percent collection of receivables that are more than 30 days overdue. Similarly, in sales collection, up-to-date collection is a key result area. It is also a key result area for Accounts. This is another case of joint accountability for results.

In production, too, it is evident that yield, a key result area, is the joint responsibility of both the Production and Quality Assurance departments, who are jointly accountable for ensuring that the required volume is produced at the required quality.

In the training example of participants applying what they learn back on the job, the Training Manager has that key result area and related target to achieve, as she is accountable to her superior and the company. Likewise, the line manager who sent his staff for training has that key result area and related target, and he is accountable to his superior as well as the company for the achievement of that return on investment in training.

So if both parties have to achieve the same results, then they have to sit down together and identify the complementary duties each has to perform to achieve the same result. The Training Manager has to ensure that participants at the training workshop acquire the skills and knowledge to be able to apply to situations on the job. During training, situations cited could be generic or simulated for participants to practice in and gain insights from. The line manager, on the other hand, will have to identify or provide real work situations for the returning participants to apply what they have learned, to follow up, and if necessary, to provide coaching on the job.

Transfer of training to the workplace is often neglected, which is why most companies do not derive many returns on their investment in training. Paul took me up on this point: "Sometimes, the line managers cannot perform on-the-job coaching," he argued, "because they do not have the necessary expertise!"

This is a valid argument, to which I would say that it is better to regard training and development as a means to an end, rather than as an end or activity in itself. People who apply what they have learned do so because the workplace environment supports that. To create that supportive environment, it is better to train to implement a system, a process, or a structure. The question of the manager not being able to coach will not be an issue as they would have been trained to implement the system too and part of the training would enable them to be able to coach direct reports.

As a final point on joint accountability, Sally suggested: "To ensure that both parties meet their targets for collections, for example, Sales and Accounts could get together to see who would raise the alert when an account is near overdue, who would inform the customer, and who would collect. I think it's important to be clear about our roles."

What Sally said actually touches on the nature of delegation. All the job functions people perform are delegated functions. For example, there will be a list of duties associated with collections; namely, alerting, informing and collecting. These are complementary roles to ensure that the targeted collections can be achieved and clear decisions must be made as to who is to alert, who is to inform, and who is to collect.

So, to a large extent, joint accountability results areas require teamwork and foster inter-functional working relationships. Roles must be clearly defined to avoid role conflicts when results are not achieved and shared glory when results are attained.

Henry summarized this section of the training session very neatly: "We can have very neat, balanced key results areas," he said, "but implementation requires total understanding and acceptance of the concepts and implications in other aspects of our work. Only then can people see the big picture and not be myopic about target setting. This has implications for teamwork and not just delegation."

GETTING MEASUREMENT ACCEPTED

This set us very nicely on the road to the next consideration about performance measurement: how to get measurement accepted. I asked the participants to consider why many people are resistant or wary about measurement, even though they know it is a very useful motivator for getting things done and getting things improved.

Felix volunteered the view that it is "the fear of failure and more so when results are tied to remuneration. Those who know they are capable will want measurements to confirm their achievements. Those who are not doing well, or are unable to do well, will prefer to justify performance with activities they have undertaken.

They will tend to put forward efforts as key results areas, rather than actual results achieved.''

He felt that average or acceptable performers would be anxious or confident, depending on whether the prevailing management style was encouraging or evaluative and pressurizing when results were not met.

In light of these comments, the question then arose as to how we should look at measurement, so that our concept of it is transmitted to the workforce for them to embrace it as a personal feedback tool rather than as some management action to be anxious about.

Henry was the first to respond: "If we use performance measurement as a control tool, and we use it as a carrot and stick, then employees are more likely to view it as being intimidating," he said. "However, if our objective is to give performers a tool to measure their own performance, just as a jogger would use a stopwatch to measure his workout, then no-one should feel anxious about it. In other words, we should sell it on the notion that it is for self-control, rather than for management control."

Frank took up the subject, approaching it from his particular area of expertise: "When we develop a budget, we track variances using the items in the budget as targets. That is managerial planning and control. But that is easily accepted because we are measuring the performance of the organization and there is no threat to personal esteem or face. However, if we use it as a device to track the performance of individual departments, it is like monitoring their performance. We notice that departments that do not perform well generally display signs of defensiveness. There is a personal stake and their discomfort level is higher. It's the same with individual or personal targets."

After a short silence, he continued: "If self-control is the emphasis, then the reporting of actual results versus the expected results of the individual should be viewed as providing information on progress. In that way, people would view measurement in a less intimidating light. But this is easier said than done. People will still be anxious about being measured, except when they themselves are responsible for measuring their own performance."

The managers had put it very well. There should be ownership of the results expected, and the notion of running a business within a business puts employees in the entrepreneurial chair, and the variances between expected and actual results are just updates for himself or his shareholders and stakeholders.

While there will still be some who will feel uneasy with having to measure their own performance, others will be very eager to do so. The task of management is to get the critical mass in between these two groups to be comfortable with it.

PITFALLS TO AVOID IN ESTABLISHING PERFORMANCE MEASURES

In the course of our discussions, a recent proposal by hospitals in Britain to pay National Health Service surgeons bonuses based on the number of lives they saved was brought up. This plan proposed to link the surgeons' merit payments to such things as patient mortality, rates of infection, re-admission, and post-operative mobility.

Newspaper reports on the proposal indicated that this would have the effect of deterring doctors from taking on higher-risk patients, such as the frail and the elderly, and from carrying out complex operations. Patients facing surgery were reported to be horrified by the proposals, and they questioned why doctors should be paid a premium for performing a basic duty; that is, to save lives. They felt that dedicated doctors would be insulted by the notion that they would only do their best on the operating table if there was extra money in it.

This is a classic case of measuring A and getting B, a perverted outcome that was never intended when the target was set. It is an aberration of the premise that anything measured gets done and improved. If these measures were to be implemented, the majority of doctors would perform fewer complex and risky operations.

The question arises then as to whether it is possible to refine the measurement system to prevent B from happening. In this case, quality was to be measured by the mortality rates, complications, and other clinical standards. They should perhaps have added a further quality measure—the proportion of normal and high-risk patients cared for. This could perhaps give greater rewards to doctors who care for a larger proportion of high-risk patients. Indeed, where greater recognition was accorded such cases, skillful doctors would be more likely to want to take them on.

The participants raised other, similar, examples of how quality of results might be defined differently. Felix, for example, pointed out that schools were at one time measured and ranked according to the percentage of passes their pupils attained, as well as the number of distinctions, credits, and passes scored. "This caused some school principals to be reluctant to take in weaker students," he said. "They forgot that their mission is to provide education to all who need it. The key results areas for schools have since been refined to include factors like level of improvement by the school. This gives recognition to schools that take in weaker students and enable them to learn better. So this is another way of defining quality of results."

Having considered these general examples from outside the company's field, Sally brought the discussion back to the specifics of Resu's activities and to her specific area: "In sales, many companies used to reward salespeople on gross sales revenue alone. As a result, salespeople worked hard to inflate sales volume and value to earn large commissions. But when quality measures—like the mix of new and old customers, and new and established products—were included, the payment of commissions was no longer just based on sales revenue or volume alone, and the better, more professional salespeople were revealed."

Summing up the above discussions, we were able to conclude that individual measures have to be comprehensive, and take into consideration quantity, time, quality, cost, and human reaction and impact. It may be more difficult and time-consuming to derive standards for quality and human reaction and impact, but these factors indicate the performer's level of professionalism.

Another pitfall to avoid is the way of stating measures. Businesses tend to establish negative measures such as resignation or turnover rate instead of positive ones like retention rate. They use reject rate rather than acceptance rate. They measure downtime rather than uptime, and so on. Yet another common pitfall to which many fall foul is that of confusing result with action. This could be because they are more action-oriented than results-oriented.

Sally pointed out that sometimes results look a lot like desired actions. "For example," she said, "a sales manager may have a target to launch a promotion campaign to generate more sales. Which is the target and which is the action? Both can be actions and both can be a key result area." In such a case, we have to look at one as an end, and the other as a means to an end. For that sales manager, the desired result could be to generate sales of a certain amount by year-end. The promotion campaign would be the means to achieve that end, or the action to take.

To launch a promotion campaign by a certain date would perhaps be a target for the Advertising and Promotion Manager. That would be his end and his means would be to select media reach, arrange the event venue, offer promotional incentives, and so on.

Paul, who had clearly been mulling over what had been said about the tendency to accentuate the negative aspects of measurement, had another perspective. "I am also asking myself whether measuring accident rates is enough to reduce accidents in the workplace, because accident rates are available only after the fact," he said. "Should we not also measure things that can help prevent accidents, such as housekeeping? Machine maintenance is already handled by Engineering to prevent accidents from machinery operations. So we should measure the preventive besides the corrective, shouldn't we?"

Eugene agreed: "I'd say it's better to measure the preventive than the corrective. It's cheaper and safer. How about also measuring near-misses like crates dropping from forklift trucks, people slipping and nearly falling on wet floors, etc.?"

These were very good suggestions and a further preventive measure may be the number of hazard hunts done per week. It might also be good to measure improvements instead of compliance. For example, it is better to measure improvements in delivery times, rather than simply concentrating on late deliveries.

Henry had another contribution about pitfalls to avoid. "We often take measures but we seldom act on them promptly after the results are known. Also, we tend to act only on the negative variances. Shouldn't we congratulate those who achieve positive variances and learn from their successes too? That is the human side of measurement. It is not about figures and statistics. It is about people and performance."

At this point, Frank added: "In Finance and Accounting, there's no such thing as a perfect measure. It is what is universally acceptable. That is also why we have so many sets of measures to measure the financial health of an organization. Yet some organizations have been able to conceal their financial ill-health. Also, many stock analysts have been proven wrong in analyzing the investment values of some stocks using financial measures and other projections. Hence, there is no such thing as a perfect measure."

Martin then weighed in. "It all boils down to the question of how accurate the measures should be. For example, if we want to measure customer satisfaction, we could commission a detailed survey among our customers. But every survey by a specialist agency costs money and time, and we may not be able to do this regularly. Besides, these surveys use random sampling and not 100 percent samples."

We cannot hope to measure everything accurately all the time. We can, for example, accept compliments over complaints as a valid indirect measure of the level of customer satisfaction.

The same would apply for employee morale, or what is sometimes referred to as "organizational climate." We cannot possibly conduct a survey every month to monitor employee morale, but we could use indirect measures such as punctuality, absenteeism rate, and retention rate, which are symptomatic of morale. These may not be 100 percent accurate, but they are acceptable measures. For business purposes, using what is practical, acceptable, and cost-effective to collect will often have to suffice. Some personality inventories and profiling instruments have also been regarded as having face validity. Yet, they are accepted as additional data to provide a composite picture of someone's personality make-up.

Indirect measures are acceptable so long as they are understood and accepted. In fact, it is safe to assert that there is no such thing as a measure with 100 percent accuracy and validity. For example, a panel of judges at a beauty contest will be an indirect measure of beauty. Some people might dispute the judgments, but they are accepted measures, unless we can come up with more-direct and less-cumbersome measures.

Applications

In training sessions, I usually ask participants to try setting targets for their professional/technical functions and/or their managerial functions. As a guide, I show them an example of a training manager's technical and managerial functions, as illustrated in Figure 2.3.

Figure 2.3. The Training Manager's Technical and Managerial Functions

---

Training Manager's Professional and Managerial Functions

| Professional/Technical Functions |

P 1.0   Needs Analysis – Focus for this year: Competency Models
P 2.0   Induction – Focus for this year: Induction Program Revision
P 3.0   Program Development – Focus for this year: Supervisory Training
P 4.0   Evaluation – Focus for this year: Coaching by Line Managers

| Managerial Functions |

M 1.0   Communication – Focus for this year: Weekly Meetings
M 2.0   Staffing – Focus for this year: Job Description of New Training Executive
M 3.0   Subordinate Training – Focus for this year: Creativity Applications
M 4.0   Working Relations – Focus for this year: Resolve Roles in Departments

---

In apportioning targets between the two sets of functions, as a rule of thumb, the higher the managerial position held, the more managerial functions there should be relative to professional/technical functions.

The relative percentages have to be agreed on between the manager and his/her superior. If the organization is young or a start-up, even senior managers may spend more time and attention on professional/technical functions to get the business going.

To end the session, I then showed the relative weighting between professional/technical work and managerial work on a hierarchical matrix (see Figure 2.4).

Figure 2.4. Relative Weighting Between Professional/Technical and Managerial Functions

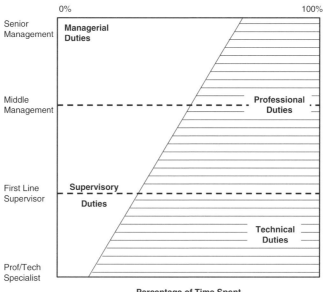

Percentage of Time Spent

Key Points to Ponder

- Things measured do not automatically get done or improved.
- An appropriate organizational culture is needed to foster commitment to specific results desired.
- Intentions and expectations need to be translated into specific results desired. This process needs to be learned so that every functional contribution can be measured.
- The SMART criteria have their limitations in assisting all functional groups to establish performance measures.

(continued)

- The thinking process for establishing performance measures goes from identifying critical and key results areas, to creating key performance indicators as units of measure, to target setting.
- A balanced set of individual performance measures will include measures of efficiency and effectiveness.
- Measuring efficiency takes into consideration quantity and time—how much and by when certain quantities (in volume or value) have to be achieved.
- Measuring effectiveness takes into consideration quality, cost, and human reaction or impact—how well the efficiency has been achieved (the quality of the quantitative results achieved, the cost incurred, and the positive or negative impact of the results achieved on people).
- Managerial performance should be measured, in addition to technical or operational performance.
- Targets need to be challenging and achievable to motivate people to contribute to productivity.
- Every step in a product/service-delivery process can have balanced measures, so that everyone knows he is virtually operating a business within a business. The person in the next step is the internal customer who serves the ultimate external customer.
- Pitfalls to avoid in establishing performance measures include: confusing actions with results; being mindful of unexpected outcomes that pervert or diminish the importance of the original results desired; and using performance measures as a carrot-and-stick approach.
- It is important to get measurement accepted before implementation, as measurement can be intimidating even to conscientious workers.

CHAPTER THREE

PERFORMANCE MANAGEMENT AND REVIEW

Managing for commitment, not just for compliance

Implementing a Results-Management System

Achieving Results through and with People

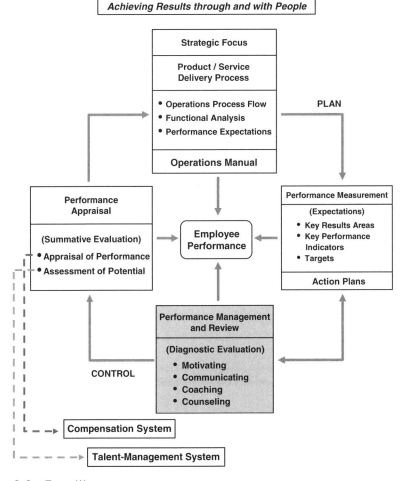

© Ong Teong Wan

CONVINCING PEOPLE AND MOVING PEOPLE

One of my worldly-wise workshop participants once said: "Logic and reason may convince people, but emotions move people."

He was telling his friends in the same workshop that to achieve productivity gains, it was necessary to win people's hearts (and not only their minds) to a new way of working; that is, to be more results-focused rather than just activity-focused. He said that winning minds over the necessity for logically balanced sets of individual targets was not enough to ensure commitment to achieving the desired results.

How wise he was, and that is the inspiration for this chapter on performance management, to enable line managers to achieve desired results through and with people. It is the heartbeat of a results-management system.

BASIC MANAGERIAL FUNCTIONS REVISITED

After the workshop on performance measurement, the participants went back to their respective divisions and departments to plan how they were going to set targets for themselves first.

It had been thought that setting targets was easy, and getting understanding and acceptance was the only difficult part. Now the participants realized that the expected results also had to be balanced; simply measuring quantity and time was not enough.

Identifying key results areas is the hard-thinking and focused part, from which key performance indicators and targets would logically flow. Key results areas reflect the value system of the people who regard them as key or, in some instances, as critical.

Listing the professional/technical functions and identifying key results areas are not difficult, but most managers have difficulty listing their managerial functions. Referring to standard management reference books may help.[1] These would probably list some of the following as basic functions and key competencies:

Planning and Controlling: *Forecasting; Strategic Planning; Action Planning; Budgeting; Establishing Performance Measures; Measuring; Evaluating and Correcting Performance; Establishing Policies and Procedures.*

Organizing: *Designing Organization Structures; Establishing Functional Roles and Relationships; Delegating.*

Leading: *Identifying, Recruiting, Selecting and Retaining Talent; Coaching and Counseling; Appraising Performance and Potential; Problem Solving; Decision Making; Communicating; Motivating.*

The task of establishing key results areas for a range of managerial competencies might seem formidable to managers and may meet with resistance from them, especially as they also have a fair amount of professional/technical work to pay attention to. This was certainly the case at Resu Co., where some of the departments were fairly new and, with some fresh graduates and inexperienced professional/technical personnel recently taken on, the depth of professional/technical know-how was not well embedded.

However, measuring managerial performance is as vital as measuring professional/technical performance and talent needs to be well-managed. Talent management and retention are critical to business competitiveness and success.

The list of basic functions and key competencies outlined above was presented to the participants at the beginning of the training workshop on performance management. After reviewing this, Tracy asked how she should prioritize the managerial functions to be measured, as every managerial function seemed important.

Tracy was advised to identify the critical few managerial functions for the year, bearing in mind the relative weighting for professional/technical work based on the person's level of management. This would have to be agreed between the managers and their immediate superiors, or the people they supervise.

For example, one of Tracy's immediate key managerial functions for the year would be to implement the results-management system under the key management function of Leading, all the competencies for which would have to be applied. Implementing the results-management system would in itself cover many basic managerial functions from Planning and Controlling to Leading.

Henry made the point that staff retention should be a standard key result area for the Leading function, because talented people represented the company's intellectual capital, which included not only knowledge, skills, intellectual property and other organizational assets, but also the business relationships that key personnel have established with suppliers and customers over the years.

Frank supported the idea. From his experience in the Finance Division, he said, "When people leave, most of the time there are internal push factors which we may or may not be aware of. These are accelerated by pull factors from outside."

This is certainly true, particularly in an Asian context, where exit interviews do not reveal much when people may not want to be forthright about their true reasons for leaving. In the same way, dissatisfied customers often leave without comment, except for a few vocal or really incensed ones who will voice their displeasure loudly and widely.

People are generally creatures of habit, and they usually do not want to leave a comfort zone, especially one in which they enjoy job satisfaction, caring superiors, a mutually supportive work environment and a just and adequate reward system.

MANAGING FOR COMMITMENT, NOT JUST FOR COMPLIANCE

At the workshop on performance management subtitled "Managing for Commitment, Not Just for Compliance," the results-management system diagram was again projected on the screen, this time with the Performance Management and Review box highlighted.

Performance reviewing is a process of periodically reviewing the actual results achieved against the targets set. During periodic results reviews, performance management skills in motivation and communication are needed to build a trusting working relationship for diagnosing performance problems. Performance coaching and counseling are needed if the actual results deviate from results that should have been achieved. Deviations from targets have to be diagnosed and corrected there and then—and not at appraisal time.

Periodic Results Reviewing is evaluation in a diagnostic sense, and Performance Appraisal is a summative evaluation of final results achieved.

As a lead-in, I quickly recapitulated the key learning points on performance measurement from the previous workshop:

Things measured may get things done most of the time, but anything measured would only be improved if performance management was also part of the results-oriented culture.

It requires only compliance to get things done. To get things done well (or improved) requires commitment. A natural passion to get things improved and done well is usually confined to a small group of people. Commitment is possible from more people if they are managed well.

On the flip chart, I wrote this phrase:

Manage for Commitment, not just for Compliance.

There are some basic managerial competencies that many managers talk about and management gurus write about, but many have yet to do much about. These are often labeled as soft skills, which often connote nice-to-know skills rather than need-to-master skills.

I also wrote: **What Turns Us On** and **What Turns Us Off** and asked participants to recall experiences they may have had as direct reports where what superiors did or said turned them on or off at work. Not surprisingly, it was the turn-offs that received the greatest response because, as someone said, turn-offs are more common, and so it is easier to list them.

The lists the four groups came up with were more or less identical in content, although not in exact words or phrases. I have asked the same set of questions with many groups—from technicians, clerical assistants, secretaries, junior executives, professionals, to senior managers and directors—and most of them have come up with more or less the same conclusions, as follows on Page 44.

What does this tell us about people? It tells us that people can be different in position, wealth level, gender, age, job functions, educational levels, and so on, but they are also the same in that they are turned on and off by the same behaviors and actions of those who supervise them, report to them, work with them, or interact with them.

Asked for a possible explanation as to why, invariably, it was the same few recurring actions or behaviors that turned people on and off, Henry suggested that they all involved people's feelings, particularly regarding their need to feel important. The group nodded their agreement.

Turn-Ons	
(1) shows appreciation gives recognition pat on the back praise for good work gives credit when due rewards in words and in kind	(2) understanding and helpful develops and coaches corrects without hurting gives useful feedback when a mistake is made encouraging
(3) open and receptive listens to you open-minded accepts criticisms hears you out interested in what you have to say	(4) understanding and frank accepts your viewpoints can empathize with you does not only think of himself always tries to resolve issues looks at the big picture

Turn-Offs	
(1) steals credit unappreciative brags about own achievements never a good word for you stingy with praise	(2) good at fault-finding reprimands freely makes discouraging remarks puts you down uptight when mistakes are made
(3) interrupts when you speak closed-minded only wants to be heard never listens in one ear, out the other	(4) always wants to win a point cares more for self than for others doesn't try to understand others adopts a win-lose attitude unsympathetic and inconsiderate

This certainly fits in with the motivational theory on higher-order needs for esteem, or the ego need. They also refer to an innate desire in most of us to perform well. This goes back to basics on human relations, founded on basic communication skills and motivation fundamentals. These are being re-visited in current popular management literature under interesting and arresting labels. How relevant these management behaviors are to the achievement of targets will become clearer later. For now, it is sufficient to note that they help to develop a trusting working relationship.

GIVING CREDIT

The participants were then asked to consider the following scenario:

> *At about 4:30 one afternoon John, an executive, was tasked with writing a report for a meeting scheduled for 9:00 the following morning. The assignment required him to go through many hardcopy files dating back a number of years to obtain data for the report. He stayed till late into the night to complete the report, classifying and tabulating the data properly for easy reference. He submitted the report to his superior at 8:30a.m. the following day.*
>
> *John heard that the meeting went well and the report was very useful in helping the meeting to promptly arrive at a decision.*

I asked the participants to put themselves in John's shoes and to describe their feelings or possible reactions if, after the meeting: (a) their superior said nothing about it; (b) someone else who had been at the meeting complimented them on the excellent and well-documented report; (c) the superior said to them "Good job. Well done"; or (d) their superior said immediately afterwards, "Thanks, John, for getting the report in first thing. I know I didn't give you much time. Despite that, you got all the data assembled for easy reference, which enabled us to arrive at a quick decision."

Interestingly, the participants gave slightly different reactions in the various responses to John's work.

For example, for (a), one group wrote and underscored: "No news is good news." One of the group had had an experience in a previous workplace where his superior only ever spoke to him if something had gone wrong, or performance was not up to expectations. Good performance was never discussed, as this was expected. Hence, no news was good news.

Another group wrote: "We would feel disappointed. We wouldn't know whether the report was useful or not." They explained that they thought they had done a good job, but there was no confirmation. The silence got them wondering whether the report had been acceptable.

The third group wrote: "This is normal and OK. So long as I know I did a good job, I am satisfied. I don't need anyone to pat me on the back." This, however, was not the response of the majority of the group, who, in fact, felt that they would be disheartened. The answer they gave reflected the feelings of one of the more self-confident members, who wanted this possible reaction to be presented.

The fourth group wrote: "We would feel taken for granted. Next time, we wouldn't try so hard, but just do the minimum required." This group explained that since good performance was inconsequential, they wouldn't bother to go all out the next time.

From these reactions—all of which were equally feasible—it is possible to extrapolate the following points.

In this scenario, if the majority of people in an organization said "no news is good news," they would generally be risk avoiders. They would concentrate on avoiding mistakes, instead of doing well or better. Good performance would be taken for granted and poor performance would be highlighted.

For the group that felt disappointed and unsure as to whether they had done well, theirs would be an understandable reaction. Some might be prompted to ask the superior how the report had been received, even though they might already have heard it on the grapevine.

Those who assert that they do not need confirmation of their good work would undoubtedly be in the minority. Such self-assured individuals would continue to do what they thought had to be done, according to their own standards.

The group that felt taken for granted and reacted by deciding to do the minimum in future would perform just to comply, and their commitment level would generally be low.

From this scenario, the impact of a lack of positive feedback on the performer's behavior is clear. Giving/not giving credit when due can have important ramifications for future motivation.

The workshop next reviewed the possible reactions to scenario (b), in which someone other than John's superior complimented him on the report. Here, the reactions ranged from "Pleased and satisfied—as long as someone recognized the effort, that would be enough" to "We would be happy and encouraged if this person were someone senior or, better still, our boss's superior" to "We would feel encouraged, but disappointed with our boss for not recognizing our efforts" to "We would be motivated and willing to forgive our boss if he is usually appreciative. Perhaps he had good reasons for not saying anything this time."

Without further comment, we moved on to the third scenario, in which the superior simply said, "Good job. Well done." Here, while the acknowledgment was generally appreciated, some were somewhat cynical about the response: "It doesn't sound sincere," one group said; "maybe he just needs us to do another report." By contrast, the fuller response in scenario (d) drew much more animated responses: "We would be on Cloud Nine" . . . "We would gladly do the next report and even improve on the presentation."

From this, we were able to draw clear ideas about the nature of giving credit, which I then summarized on the flipchart:

Giving credit is describing what you like about someone's performance or suggestion.

Being descriptive rather than evaluative in giving feedback—positive or negative—has more credibility and is more effective.

Giving credit where it's due reinforces good performance, and makes people want to repeat the same good experience.

I wrote a simple formula on the flipchart to explain this:

performance = willingness + ability

Willingness has to do with a person's attitude—a want-to or don't-want-to attitude. Ability has to do with a person's skills and knowledge—the can-do or cannot-do.

Giving credit for good performance creates a willingness to repeat the same performance. It is also telling the performer that he has done something in the correct way (using his skills and knowledge) to achieve positive results or meet expectations.

Although aptitude—an innate ability to learn a particular knowledge area or skill quickly—features in a person's performance, performing well is still determined largely by the attitude or willingness to perform.

As we have seen, to give credit effectively it must be specific about what was done that deserved the credit. It needs to refer to the actions taken or the attitude shown. Above all, the usefulness or value of the action or performance needs to be alluded to.

It has to be given when performance or a suggestion exceeds expectations or targets, and even when a person consistently meets expectations. People who perform well on a consistent basis need to be reminded from time to time that they are not being taken for granted. In such cases, though, it must not come across as being perfunctory praise and a specific reference to the actions and their value will still mean much to the performer.

I sketched the following graph mapping the performance of a newcomer who was just learning his job. I asked the class to consider what they would do if this person were in their area of responsibility.

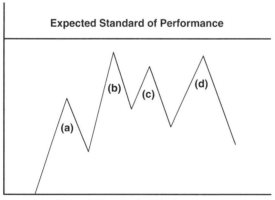

While his performance had improved, he was still below the expected standard. Would they give him credit for the improvements he'd made?

Felix felt that credit should be given to encourage him: "If we don't say anything, he will not feel encouraged. Learning something new can be difficult, and there will be more failures than successes.''

On the other hand, Tracy felt that while giving credit would encourage him, it could also convey the wrong idea that the standard of work was acceptable. Superiors needed to convey clearly the standards expected. Giving credit in this situation would send the wrong signal.

This led us naturally to the next competency: how to give constructive feedback when performance was below expectation.

But before moving on, it's worth reminding ourselves that the need to give credit applies equally across the board, to superiors as well as direct reports. Whenever, wherever and by whomever a job is done well—including by supervisors, suppliers, peers and customers—due credit needs to be given and in a timely fashion, rather than as an afterthought. Doing so will foster a healthy and positive work environment.

CONSTRUCTIVE FEEDBACK

I commenced this session with an incident that actually happened in one organization.

The Marketing Director of a consumer-products company had just finished a meeting to change the company's price list, and rushed off to meet a client.

While he was out, a customer called his office for a price list. The call was received by his secretary, who promptly arranged for the dispatch clerk to deliver the existing price list to the customer.

When the Marketing Director returned after lunch, his secretary informed him of what she had done.

I asked the groups to discuss how the Marketing Director might react to being told that she had sent the outdated price list. Their responses were as follows:

1. ''Oh dear. Next time you had better check before sending out price lists. The one you sent was out of date. We just revised it this morning.''

2. "Big problem. The price list you sent out was not current. We revised it this morning."

3. "I think next time you should let the sales people handle the price lists. They will know the latest. Now we have to honor the old prices with this customer. I hope other customers don't get to hear about it, or we'll have a headache."

4. "I like it that you took the initiative to respond to the customer promptly. That is part of our service culture. But what you sent out was the old price list. We just updated it this morning. Sorry I had to rush off and had no chance to tell you. What can we do about it?"

I then asked them to respond to each of these scenarios as if they were the secretary. Their responses to the first included:
- "I'd keep quiet."
- "I'd retort that I was just trying to be a helpful member of the marketing team."
- "Someone should have told me it had been revised."

The responses to the second scenario produced another set of defensive answers:
- "Losing a customer is a bigger problem."
- "Nobody told me. Do I have to pay for it?"
- "Next time I won't touch it."

For the third scenario, they presented the following responses:
- "Okay, next time I will mind my own business."
- "I hope they do know, especially when they are out all the time."
- "Isn't customer service everyone's business in this organization?"

As expected, reactions in the final scenario were less defensive and more constructive:
- "We could put a note on every price list in future to remind users to confirm its validity before sending out."
- "Let me see if I can intercept the dispatch clerk."
- "I'm sorry. I should have checked first before sending it out."

The group's responses to the way the manager reacted to the error were quite common. In the first three scenarios, the performer was naturally defensive as the feedback was negative; the superior was putting the blame on the secretary. In the last scenario, encouraging things were said, even though the mistake had to be pointed out. It was tactfully done. Giving constructive feedback made the performer less defensive.

To summarize, then:

Constructive feedback is feedback intended to improve someone's performance or suggestion; it is not to chastise, reprimand, take to task, or mock someone whose performance or suggestion is below expectation.

Whenever we perform below expectations or make a mistake, the natural tendency is to be defensive and protect ourselves or our ego. We will usually not concentrate on correcting the error first. If our defensiveness can be reduced, we can focus on correcting the mistake. The idea is to state *what* went wrong and not *who* was wrong. The focus is on the behavior and not on the personality.

Returning for a moment to the two main variables affecting performance—willingness and ability—we learn that to create a willingness to improve, something positive about the action must be stated first before the fault or deficiency is pointed out.

In the fourth of the scenarios above, the Marketing Director stated the secretary's initiative and service mindset (the pluses) first. Then he went over the demerit or minus (the sending out of the wrong price list). Highlighting the minus is being fair yet firm about mistakes. It is descriptive rather than evaluative. This is constructive feedback.

Finally, having pointed out the error, it is necessary to look for a solution. First, a corrective action has to be taken. Then, preventive actions have to be considered, so that the same mistake does not recur. More importantly, who should ensure that the corrective and preventive actions are taken in the above scenario?

Henry felt that since the Marketing Director had asked what *they* could do about it, this indicated that he also accepted accountability for the error. At the same time, he was trying to elicit a solution from the secretary. This subtly implied that she should also assume ownership of the problem. That, to him, was the art of management—to encourage the performer to want to take remedial action and accept ownership of the problem.

I couldn't agree more. Indeed, most superiors instinctively feel the need to provide the solution, sometimes under the mistaken notion that this will gain them respect. But there are a number of advantages in eliciting a solution from the performer. Firstly, the direct report is generally nearer the action, and solutions will likely be closer to the ground to be effective. (In this incident, in fact, the secretary was able to call the dispatch clerk on his mobile phone and halt the delivery, thus averting a potential problem at the operational level. It was her solution to a problem she had unwittingly created.)

Secondly, when you encourage an employee to think of a solution, you are encouraging initiative in the performer. To do otherwise would be to risk creating a crutch mentality that all problems needed to be solved higher up, and that the solution will have to be complied with. That is the difference between managing for commitment and managing for compliance.

There will be times—perhaps when the performer is new or inexperienced—when the superior has to provide the solution. Even then, the performer may be able to contribute a fresh perspective and it might still be worthwhile resisting the temptation to provide the answer too readily.

Even if you have an alternative solution, it is still better to go through the process before proffering your solution. This will be a reiterative process until there is consensus, understanding and acceptance of a final solution or combination of solutions. This makes it easier to implement the solution, as there is involvement from the implementer.

But for some newly promoted managers such an approach is not always easy to effect and Eugene was able to share his own experience in this regard:

"I recall being promoted above my peers in a high-tech firm. All of us were specialists in our own areas, but once you were made manager, you became a generalist overnight. When there were technical problems beyond your technical experience, you might not have the technical depth to solve them. If you tried to be clever by trying to provide answers, or tried to show who was the boss, you were in for a lot of support and commitment issues.

"Eventually, I realized it was better to be honest and admit humbly that I did not have all the answers, and that my staff specialists would be the ones who could provide solid answers.

"Initially I was afraid that they would think that my role was irrelevant, and that gave me a lot of stress and anxiety. But then I thought it through, and I decided I had to distinguish between process and content. I realized that my role as a manager was to point out what was or was not working, or what aspect was done right or not done right. That, I think, is the constructive feedback process for correcting a poor outcome. The specialists under my charge should deal with the content and be motivated to provide the creative solutions."

In this case, Eugene managed to win the respect and co-operation of his former peers (who became his direct reports) by using the constructive-feedback process and allowing his direct reports to provide the solution. He had managed to sort out their complementary roles, which is the essence of teamwork leadership.

As we have seen, the constructive-feedback process requires that the one providing that feedback is able to state the merits of the action in order to reduce defensiveness on the part of the performer while, at the same time, describing the demerits to highlight the need for improvement.

But what happens if you cannot see any merit in the action that has been taken? This was a point raised by Frank: "I like the process. I can see that it's logical and motivating. But sometimes, for the life of me, I cannot see any merit or plus in what people do or say. I'm not proud to say it, but my immediate impulse is to point out the demerit. If I try to say something like 'What you did was good, but . . . ,' it would seem hypocritical, especially when what was done was idiotic! How are we supposed to state a merit or plus when we cannot see any?"

I threw it open to the group. Martin suggested that: "The easiest way might be to ask the performer why he did something that way. What merit or advantage did he see? We could say something tactful like, 'I'm not sure I understand the advantages of your proposal. Would you like to elaborate on it before I give my comments?'"

Several in the group nodded in agreement.

Yes, ask the performer. They will have a rationale for the things they do or say. We do not see the pluses the same way they see them. If we insist that they see things our way, that is, the minus or minuses, they may become defensive or resistant. So let's look at things their way first, before trying to bring them around to seeing things our way.

Dealing with performance deficiencies in this manner not only increases the chances of gaining the respect and co-operation of those you supervise, but is also likely to instill confidence in your direct reports. People who are less worried about making mistakes are likely to learn more on the job, to innovate without fear of blame if things go wrong, and to initiate solutions for greater productivity.

EFFECTIVE LISTENING

To begin the next session at Resu Co., I opened with the following scenario, and asked the participants how managers might react in this instance.

A conscientious administrative assistant had an idea to improve office productivity. He made this suggestion to his manager: "Boss, I think we should centralize our filing system for easy retrieval of files."

The groups were asked to discuss and list common responses to this suggestion, and they came up with the following possibilities:

1. "We've been storing files like this for years and it has served us well. I really don't see the need for change. Thanks for the suggestion anyway."
2. "Good idea. Go ahead and do it."
3. "How much will it cost?"
4. "Talking about files, we need to have the budget files available for our meeting tomorrow."
5. "I see. What do you have in mind specifically?"

I then asked them which of these indicated that the manager had been listening.

Someone suggested that respondents 1, 2 and 3 were listening, as they were reacting to the suggestion. Respondent 4 was obviously not listening as he changed the subject. Respondent 5 was just curious to know more. This prompted a discussion on what we actually mean by "listening."

Effective Listening is actively searching for the meaning of what people are trying to say and why they are saying it. This is more than is implied in the well-known phrase "active listening" because how accurately or effectively we understand a message is crucial.

By that definition, therefore, respondents 1, 2 and 3 could not be said to be listening. They were reacting, and they were assuming that they knew exactly what the speaker had in mind and why he was suggesting it. In fact, respondent 1 was dismissive and did not bother to find out more about what was being suggested. Respondent 2 assumed he knew exactly what the assistant had in mind, and gave the go-ahead. After all, the assumption seems to be, wasn't it just a matter of re-arranging and shifting filing cabinets to a central location in the office?

Respondent 3, too, assumed he knew what was entailed and merely asked for the cost.

As most of the group were quick to point out, respondent 4 was obviously not listening and simply changed the subject.

Respondent 5 was the one good listener. He was trying to find out more about the "what" and the "why" of the proposal. He was not dismissive. He did not assume he knew exactly what the speaker was trying to say, and he wanted to know more. He had, in a sense, accorded value to what the speaker was trying to say. In the list of turn-ons discussed earlier, he would be seen as approachable, receptive, open-minded and interested in the direct report as a person.

Good listeners therefore make people feel important and recognized. They are more likely to obtain more information, and they themselves will likely get to be heard too.

I posed another scenario for the class.

You are at a staff meeting to discuss candidates for a job vacancy. Job specifications have been discussed. Some names were suggested. Some could be considered. Others, it was unanimously concluded, were clearly unsuitable.

Up to now, there has been no conclusive agreement on a suitable candidate. Then someone remarked, "Let's consider people from other departments as well."

This time, the participants were asked for their interpretations of this remark. These were their responses:

- The speaker wants to give everyone in the organization a chance.
- The speaker has someone in mind.
- The speaker does not agree with the names mentioned.
- The speaker favors recruiting from within the organization.
- The speaker prefers candidates from other departments.
- The speaker believes in casting the net as widely as possible.

These were all interesting and, indeed, plausible interpretations. But, short of having extra-sensory or telepathic powers to read people's thoughts behind their utterances, there can be no real certainty as to which, if any, of these is correct. People don't always say what they mean. Sometimes, intentionally or otherwise, neither do they always mean what they say. And often we only hear what we want to hear.

To ensure that we have interpreted what has been said correctly, or, for that matter, whether the speaker means what he has said, we can clarify the "what" and the "why' with the speaker. But even then we can't assume that we have understood accurately the intent behind the statement without checking back with the speaker. This is often done simply by confirming in our own words what we have heard. This is not merely a parroting of the speaker's words but a paraphrasing; that is, stating our understanding in our own words.

To summarize then; for effective listening we should not automatically assume that we have understood what has been said. To avoid that assumption, we should clarify what was said and why it was said. If we think we have understood what was said and why it was said, then we confirm our understanding by paraphrasing it back to the speaker.

Communication, whether spoken or written, is a process that involves the encoding of ideas by the speaker/writer and the decoding of those ideas by the listener/reader. For the communication to be effective, certain barriers have to be confronted and overcome, as illustrated in Figure 3.1.

When someone has an idea or concept to convey, he needs to encode it in order to transmit it to the receiver of the message. To encode is to convert the abstract concept into a written or verbal form, or a picture, symbol, signal or gesture, so that the receiver of the message can visualize and grasp the meaning intended. However, our encoding efforts are often distorted or hampered by a host of barriers—physical, psychological, cultural,

Figure 3.1. Overcoming Barriers to Communication

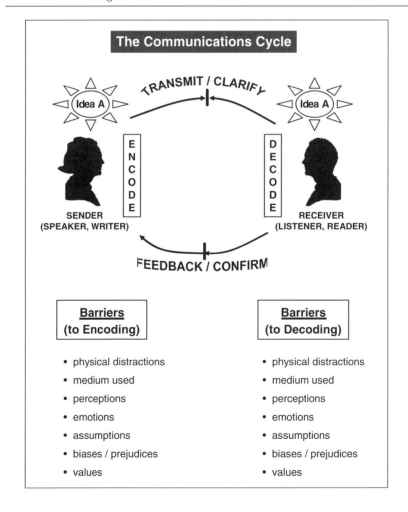

or emotional. These can include our articulation, our accents, our choice of words, our mistaken assumptions about the listener's perceptive ability, or the influence of our past interactions with the listener.

We are more practiced with sending messages, spoken or written. We often get opportunities to attend courses on writing and speaking to overcome these barriers. Receiving the message effectively, on the other hand, poses greater challenges.

In receiving messages, the receiver decodes as he listens or reads, but the decoding process may be distorted or influenced by physical, psychological, cultural, and emotional barriers as well. There might also be noise distractions affecting reception and understanding, the receiver could be preoccupied with something else, or emotions like sadness or elation could color his understanding of the message. His values and beliefs could also pose barriers to understanding as they act as filters or distorters.

We are generally less practiced and have fewer opportunities for training in receiving spoken messages. We tend to jump to conclusions or react quickly to spoken messages. Therefore, in order to overcome barriers to listening, clarifying and confirming will guide us to actively search for the meaning of what the sender is trying to convey, and why he is conveying it.

Thus, the art of listening is also the art of questioning. In seeking to clarify the what and why, you might ask:

- What did you have in mind when you said that?
- Can you elaborate on what you mean by . . . ?
- What is the intention behind that suggestion?
- Would you mind clarifying your rationale for it?

In confirming the what and the why, you might use phrases such as:

- Correct me if I'm wrong. You want to . . . . Am I right?
- So your idea is to . . . ?
- The reason behind your proposal is . . . Am I correct?
- So you are suggesting this so that we could . . . ?

The better we master the art of listening, the more we can learn about what and how others think.

However, if we had to clarify and paraphrase every statement or opinion that is made to ensure we understand clearly, life would be very tedious for both listener and speaker.

Most of the time in our day-to-day communication, we don't follow this process and we can take the risk of minor misunderstandings without serious consequences. There are occasions, however, particularly in our business and professional lives, when it is essential to follow the process to ensure effective communication.

The participants offered a range of examples from their own experience of when effective listening would be crucial. These included when dealing with grievances from employees or when the instinctive reaction may be to be defensive or to disagree with what is being said, especially if this relates to the company's policy or image. At exit interviews, too, general statements such as "morale is low" or "your salary is not competitive" or "I want a change" need to be probed further to gain better insights.

Another crucial area is in customer service, where it is not sufficient to simply apologize when things go wrong. While it is necessary to effect a quick solution to the problem this shouldn't be done without first finding out more about the cause of the customer's dissatisfaction. The effective-listening process undoubtedly elicits the kind of information that enables both corrective and preventive measures to be taken.

As highlighted in our example earlier, another situation when effective listening is vital is when dealing with suggestions from direct reports on how processes may be improved. The best decisions are made when all the information necessary to weigh up the pros and cons is available. And detailed information is obtained through effective listening.

If we can encourage suggestions from employees on an informal basis, by listening to them carefully and sincerely, we will encourage more spontaneous suggestions. They won't mind so much even if the idea is not taken up so long as it is given due consideration.

Employers/managers who really listen to what their direct reports have to say are likely to reap the benefits in commanding greater respect, commitment and loyalty.

HANDLING CONFLICT

This session opened with the following scenario:

> *The company has implemented a system of small-group activities among non-managerial staff. These activities are voluntary, and the meetings take place after office hours every Friday evening. They are intended to involve and engage employees in solving operational problems.*
>
> *These activities have been implemented in Japanese companies, and have been shown to improve productivity, cost savings, team spirit, and staff retention.*
>
> *Employees in supervisory positions must be selected to oversee these activities and facilitate the meetings. These leaders will guide and train their groups in problem-solving and creative-thinking techniques.*
>
> *All supervisory and managerial staff have attended a briefing on how the small-group activities are done. Training for the group leaders will be provided after they have been nominated.*
>
> *You approach your line supervisor to start one group. However, this supervisor is neither keen nor willing to take on the role. He says he had classes to attend on Friday evenings, and he has to fetch his children home from school as his wife is unavailable on Fridays.*

I then asked the class to consider some of the common approaches managers might take in this situation.

The groups came up with two possible approaches:

Approach 1
Arrange a private meeting with the supervisor and explain to him the importance of the project to the company. Tell him that every department must have at least one small-group activity. Stress that he is most suited to lead the group. As for his personal commitments, tell him that if there is a will there is a way. Suggest that he gets some relative to help. Assure him that he can use an assistant in the group in his absence, if he cannot get a relative to help, or when some crucial lectures cannot be missed. Ask him to think about it and get back to you in the next few days.

Approach 2
Have a drink with him. Explain the significance of the small group activities to the department. Let him know you have great

confidence in him to lead. Tell him that since the company places importance on this, his involvement will be noted in his appraisal, and be considered in promotion exercises. If he declines, top management will not take kindly to it. Ask him to help you out; tell him that he has always been helpful and his attitude has always been good.

I then asked the class which of these would have a higher degree of success in persuading the supervisor to accept the task willingly. Opinions and conclusions were varied, and they reflected the participants' past experiences in managing people.

For Approach 1, someone said, "He may not consider it seriously. Chances are, he will still be preoccupied with his own concerns and he's likely to decline."

Someone else said, "He may accept the role if he feels indebted to the manager, can get relatives to help with his children and is confident of his grades for his studies. The chances of fulfilling all that seem remote, though."

A third person thought he might be resentful of the strong "sales pitch" and pressure tactics. He might retort that it was a voluntary activity and not a contractual duty.

For Approach 2, one immediate response was, "This is the classic carrot-and-stick approach, using incentives and disincentives. Some might be coerced into submitting for fear of reprisals. There will not be much commitment if he accepts."

Another person volunteered, "This approach assumes that people are motivated by pleasure and pain alone, and there are no other needs that are more immediate and relevant to the performer."

"If this supervisor badly wants to be promoted, and he sees this as an opportunity to be noticed, then he might accept the role. What he does with the group after accepting is another matter," said a third person.

All agreed that it is very unprofessional for a manager to hint at a good appraisal and future promotion as a means of getting someone to do something he is not inclined to do. Performing one voluntary activity is not a ticket to a good appraisal or a promotion. That sends the wrong signal, and may cause more unhappiness in future. Nevertheless, such tactics are sometimes used at work (or, indeed, in the home in persuading children to do their homework or to study hard). After a while, though, these tactics lose their motivational value and the managers who employ them lose their credibility.

The groups thought they had finished discussing the merits and demerits of the two approaches, when someone raised a very interesting question: "Isn't the supervisor expected to show a good example and accept the role without even being asked? If I were his manager, I would just tell him he has to do it even though he is reluctant. Yes, it is voluntary, but as a leader he has an obligation to implement something important like this, where productivity is concerned."

This is certainly one approach open to managers but it may well not produce the intended effect. In such circumstances, is the supervisor likely to put his heart and soul into it? Will he be motivated to inspire his group to come up with creative solutions? This is managing for compliance rather than for commitment.

All of the approaches discussed are commonly used by many and, in some instances, they do work. People who may be unenthusiastic about something initially may become more enthusiastic as they get involved. Sometimes, the enthusiasm of the group may rub off on the reluctant participant. In this situation, though, we should look for an approach that increases the probability of success, or the supervisor's willing acceptance of the assignment.

On the surface, this may be seen as an exercise in persuasion or a cajoling session. In effect, though, it is an example of handling a conflict. A conflict does not always involve an open fight or an exchange of angry words. These are signs of conflict. When there is a difference in priorities (objectives, opinions, beliefs, values, and so on), a conflict can be said to exist.

Handling conflict is managing differences (of opinions, objectives, preferences, values, beliefs, and so on) in such a way that it leads to a mutually beneficial outcome or what is normally termed a win-win conclusion.

When a solution benefits both parties, it's easier to implement as there'll be a vested interest on both sides.

If, in our example, the supervisor is directed to lead the activity against his wishes, he will feel that the superior has won and he has lost. He has to sort out his children's transportation problems and he has to miss classes he has paid for. So, it won't be surprising if he does not put in his best efforts, and the small group produces nothing of any value. If that happens, neither has won. At his year-end appraisal, the superior may hold the group's dismal results against him and rate him poorly, affecting his appraisal rating and track record in the company.

He is disgruntled. Along comes an executive search consultant with an offer of higher pay. He is helped in this pull factor by an underlying push factor, and leaves a position that he has been comfortable with. He has generally worked well with his colleagues. He is going to an organization and a position that is unfamiliar, and he feels insecure. To conclude this dismal scenario, the manager loses an experienced supervisor and has to spend time and money looking for a replacement.

The final outcome may be a loss for both, although this may not be immediately apparent.

In the light of this, the class proceeded to review their versions of how they would do it differently. This was what they came up with. (They assumed that the supervisor knows the importance of the small group activities.)

Consolidated approach

Acknowledge and address his concerns. Help look for ways to solve his concerns about his children and his studies. Offer to render further assistance for other concerns he may have. Propose some compromise solutions, such as allowing him to leave in time to fetch his children (and have the group continue by itself), suggesting that he get a classmate to tape record lectures for him, or appointing an assistant leader in the group, etc.

In taking this approach, the group had done something that doesn't always happen in handling conflict; that is, thinking of the other person and their needs first. In fact, we seldom approach conflict from the other party's point of view. We sometimes overlook it, ignore it, downplay it, or even disparage it. In doing so, we are imposing our own values on others, which is not helpful if we hope to influence or persuade them.

The temptation might be to go for some kind of compromise solution that has a greater chance of being accepted quickly, thus minimizing delays and interruptions to the work schedule.

Compromises can be useful when a deadlock is reached and neither party is willing to budge. They can save time and are useful when time is limited. But if we look at compromises closely, they are actually an equal sharing of loss. Ideally, we want to go for a win-win solution. It reduces future regrets and is more enduring. Professional negotiators and arbiters earn their keep by using creative win-win solutions. While this normally takes more time, the quality of the resolution is generally much better.

One technique to try to reach a creative solution to problems is to impose artificial constraints, as in the following scenario which I use as an exercise for workshop participants.

Your immediate superior wants a report to be submitted in a week's time. From your experience, you need three weeks to do it properly, with all the necessary research, illustrations and narratives. What would you do?

Your first instinct might be to negotiate for a compromise agreement of two weeks. But, for the purposes of our illustration, the report is required for a board meeting in exactly one week's time. This being the case, there seems no way around it: it will just have to be done.

In cases such as this, I recommend imposing an artificial constraint: in this instance, by asking the groups to consider what they would do if the report was required by 9:00 the following morning.

The groups quickly came up with the following list of possible approaches:

- Work overtime
- Work through the night
- Skip dinner and work non-stop
- Enlist help from all departments that have to do with the report
- Provide only the bare essentials
- Avoid narratives but highlight main points
- Use only graphs and illustrations with brief narratives
- Provide a two-page summary instead of a full 10-page report
- Use last year's report as a template and just update the figures

From this abundance of ideas, three of the solutions were centered around time, and six were based on manpower, format, and content, rather than time. By moving away from a time paradigm and looking for win-win solutions within other paradigms, they gave themselves more options to choose from.

When we get into deadlocks or settle for compromises, it is usually because we work on past experiences and fixed, unquestioned assumptions. In this case, the fixed assumption that caused the deadlock was the time paradigm.

The Process for Handling Conflict

- Understand and accept what is important to the other person and why it is so.
- State what is important to you and explain why it is so.
- Seek creative win-win solutions.
- Obtain commitment to implement the solution agreed on.

So, in our original scenario where the company wanted the line supervisor to take responsibility for a group activity after working hours, using this process the manager would acknowledge the direct report's legitimate concerns but point out that the group activities were required to support the company's plans. Between them, they could discuss possible alternative arrangements, including questioning the assumption that the activities had to be on a Friday evening. After consulting with other members of the group, they may find that another evening would be better for all concerned.

Such examples of potential conflict occur on a daily basis within organizations of every kind and, more often that not, it is the line manager's responsibility to find solutions that work for all concerned. Such day-to-day examples might include having to deal with a usually conscientious section head who has begun arriving late to work on a regular basis; or tricky cases in which compromising might present a challenge to the company's policies and set an unwelcome precedent for the future.

In the course of my workshops, for example, participants have raised areas of potential conflict from their experience:

- How to deal with customers who ask for waiver of credit terms or for price discounts, where to do so would compromise company policy, but not to do so would threaten the sale.
- Company policy makes clear that no-one can accumulate annual leave and carry it over to the following year, or ask for cash reimbursement for unused paid leave. So what to do about a member of staff who, with the end of year approaching and with a great deal of work that has to be completed, has forgotten to use up her leave? Or the valued member of staff who requests permission to carry over some of the current year's paid leave for his once-in-a-lifetime honeymoon trip the following year?
- The company has a policy governing eligibility for car loans. The HR department receives requests for early consideration from staff who are just a few weeks shy of being eligible on the grounds that prices are rising rapidly as a result of foreign-exchange fluctuations.

Such examples put managers in a quandary. They would like to be able to help but to allow individual exceptions may set precedents that lead to a position where, in the end, policies may exist in name only; standards would become unclear and give rise to confusion.

In situations like these, managers can use the conflict-handling process by acknowledging, understanding, and accepting what's important to the direct report but stating clearly what is important to the company and explaining why it is so. This also ensures that they show enough interest to go into the details of the individual's constraints. This in itself may trigger solutions, by unobtrusively examining fixed paradigms within the policy constraints.

As line managers, they have a duty to see that policies are applied consistently. They can explain their role in policy implementation but, more importantly, can explain the rationale behind the policy. This is more likely to be understood and accepted if, in the first place, they have tried to understand what is important to the requester.

A policy is a constraint, and not varying the policy is, in a way, a win for the company but a loss for the employee. However, that constraint does not preclude the superior from helping to look for creative solutions with the direct report within the confines and constraints of the policy.

Even though using the process to resolve conflicts with satisfying win-win outcomes might take longer, the quality of the outcome, the higher commitment to implementing solutions, and the impact on the work environment far outweigh the effort put in. Furthermore, effective and respected leaders often handle conflicts in this way, as the turn-on/turn-off exercise showed.

It is important, though, not to use the process mechanically and gloss over what is important to the other party with overused and insincere expressions, such as, "I understand your situation, but . . . ," which do not adequately show the superior's understanding of what is important to the direct report. The superior must describe his understanding clearly and specifically. Indeed, both parties need to be equally clear and specific, so that both can have a clear picture of the overall situation.

In all of this, we have to avoid the tendency to provide instant or quick solutions, even when a situation does not require it. These sometimes lead to compromises or business-as-usual situations.

It is well worth remembering that research into conflict resolution has shown that forcing or win-lose approaches produce a low chance of an effective resolution; compromises or both-lose-some approaches have an even lower chance of effective resolution; and withdrawal from conflict approaches has no chance for resolution. Open problem-solving or win-win approaches, on the other hand, have a higher chance of effective resolution.

Pulling it All Together

It might be as well at this point to reflect for a moment over recent or past meetings you had attended, and consider how often you or others have responded in any of the following ways:

- Gave credit to ideas or suggestions that they liked.
- Shot down ideas or suggestions that they did not agree with.
- Said "Yes, but . . . "
- Said "That's a good idea, but . . . "
- Said "I like what you said about this issue. Its merits are . . . However, I have some reservations about . . . "
- Said "I'm not sure what you mean by . . . Could you tell me more?"
- Said "Let me see whether I've understood you correctly. You are saying that . . . and your reason is . . . Am I right?"
- Settled for compromises instead of working to come up with a win-win solution when there were conflicting priorities.

Reflecting on situations like these can help managers review common practices and pitfalls in interpersonal relations affecting commitment to work.

At the Resu workshop, this exercise prompted the following comment from Eugene: "I agree that these skills will motivate people to be more committed. However, I can't help but wonder if I might be construed as being manipulative, as I would still be trying to get people to do what I expect them to do. In other words, what is the difference between motivation and manipulation?"

Frank offered this perception: "I think if the direct report sees that the approach meets with his needs, then it is motivating and a win for him. On our part, as we use the approaches we discussed, we are more assured of a committed direct report and, perhaps, productive solutions, and that would be meeting our own need. I see it as simply a win-win for both and not a question of manipulation. It would only be so if one party wins and one party loses, knowingly or unknowingly."

This prompted Henry to recall the story of an assistant manager who was offered a promotion to take up a manager's position in another country. He received a salary increase, was given the use of a company car, and was allowed home leave twice a year. Six months into the new position, he resigned.

It later transpired that he had recently got married. He had tried to get his wife, who was pregnant, a job in the new location but was not successful. Every time he called home, he could hear how distraught and lonely his wife was. He asked for his former position back but it had been filled and he had no choice but to apply for a job with another company back home at a lower pay and position.

It was an unintended win-lose for the employee, as the company had assumed that the perks and pay rise would meet his career needs. It turned out that his real need was to be with his family and still be gainfully employed, above everything else.

In this case—and in many other cases—though the company may have acted with the best of intentions, it did so based on the assumption that it knew the individual's needs. In doing so, it overlooked his real needs. When this happens, it can sometimes result in unintentional win-lose situations, which ultimately lead to lose-lose outcomes.

All of the soft skills discussed so far are essential for on-the-job training, which is the focus of the next section on diagnosing performance problems.

Performance Coaching—Improving Skills and Knowledge

At the next session at Resu Co., I began by asking the participants why supervisors have difficulty in coaching and counseling their direct reports. After discussion within their groups, they came up with the following:

- Age gap. Hard to coach someone older than you
- Gender differences. In our Asian culture, it might be harder for women managers
- Hard to coach and counsel male colleagues
- Relationship too tense or distant between colleagues
- Lack of trust and willingness to be open
- Hard to point out mistakes and problems
- People get defensive
- Awkward to tell an adult what to do

- Don't know how to do it gently without hurting the other person's pride
- Not qualified to do so, especially counseling
- Prescriptive. Have to tell and direct

Though "coaching" and "counseling" are often used interchangeably, they are different concepts. When asked what "coaching" meant to them, participants often give various definitions based on their common understanding, including: showing how to do something; telling how to do something; and instructing/imparting skills. For "counseling," their understanding would include: guiding; advising; helping by advising; and mentoring.

But a clearer differentiation is required, as follows:

Performance Coaching is a diagnostic process of establishing the knowledge and skill deficiencies affecting good performance.

Performance Counseling is a diagnostic process focusing on attitude or willingness to change attitudes or mindsets that are negatively affecting an individual's performance or that of others.

It is important to stress here that we will be focusing on performance coaching and counseling, rather than other forms of counseling involving clinical or psychological issues. The process we will be looking at will be used to diagnose performance problems, and to establish their real causes.

Bearing in mind the simple equation of performance being a function of willingness and ability, a comparison between the two concepts is made in Table 3.1, below.

TABLE 3.1 PERFORMANCE COUNSELING AND COACHING COMPARED

Performance Coaching	Performance Counseling
Focuses on skills and knowledge enhancement	Focuses on willingness to change, or attitude-shaping
Skills needed: Constructive Feedback, Effective Listening, Conflict Handling	Skills needed: Constructive Feedback, Listening to Feelings, Conflict Handing

Similarities

Deals with individual performance problems on the job

Requires an open and trusting working relationship

Because individual coaching and counseling involve working on a one-to-one basis, interpersonal bonding and a trusting working relationship are critical to success.

The skills of giving credit, constructive feedback, effective listening, and conflict handling, if used appropriately, will help to encourage the open and trusting working climate essential for performance coaching and counseling.

At Resu, I presented the workshop with the following scenarios and asked if they would use coaching or counseling to address them.

1. A junior executive has had a customer complaint against her about her rudeness.

2. A direct report has difficulties in setting priorities for assignments.

3. A new member of staff is uncooperative.

4. An officer is frequently late in submitting required data.

5. A member of staff is always making full use of his medical leave entitlement.

For situation (1), most felt that counseling was required, as it was obviously an attitude problem. However, one group indicated that it could also be a skill problem: the junior executive may have used an inappropriate word or phrase inadvertently, and this could have been perceived to be rude by the customer. Therefore, coaching was required.

For situation (2), the groups were unanimous: it was a "don't know what and how" problem and coaching was required.

For situation (3), some groups thought that it could be an attitude or willingness problem, as it did not require skill or knowledge to be cooperative. Therefore, counseling was required. Other groups thought that it could be the new employee's lack of knowledge about certain issues in the organization that made him appear uncooperative, and coaching was called for.

There were mixed reactions to situation (4). Some managers, who had themselves been caught in situations where they could not submit data on time, argued that it was not their attitude that was causing the problem. Sometimes requests were submitted during busy periods (for example, month-end closing). At other times, the information needed was complex or the time given was simply insufficient.

For situation (5), the general opinion was that the medical-leave entitlement was generally seen as a policy. Whether people abused this entitlement or not depended very much on their value system. Some people will report to work despite a bad cold, while others would call in sick with the slightest cough. They concluded that it had to do with attitude, and would thus use counseling to address it.

One group had an interesting point to add. They remarked that reporting for work while seriously ill, for example, was also not ideal, as this person would not be able to work at his best, or he might spread the virus in the office. Counseling was also required in such situations.

Seemingly simple incidents can raise the question of whether it has to do with skill deficiency or attitude. The danger is in making a quick assumption. It is important to keep an open mind to find out more before trying to ascertain the most probable cause.

The groups were presented with a typical scenario and asked to come up with possible responses from untrained or unaware supervisors to the situation described below:

Your direct report should have set a date for the completion of his project and come back to you with it. So far, he has not done so. You have arranged for him to see you to review the status of what he has done, and to set a target date for completion.

The groups came up with these possible common queries from superiors wanting quick answers:

- Why haven't you set the target date yet? It's been some time since I last asked you to do that.
- What happened to the target date you're supposed to set for this project?

For coaching to be effective, we need to switch from the usual quick-fix adversarial approach—the superior asking why and the direct report defensively giving reasons or excuses (as illustrated in Figure 3.2).

FIGURE 3.2. QUICK-FIX APPROACHES TO PERFORMANCE PROBLEMS

Quick-fix solutions are, at best, interim solutions. They may be used to treat symptoms, but they may not reveal root causes.

Common approaches to coaching

Table 3.2 provides a list of the common approaches to coaching, highlighting the pros and cons of each approach.

TABLE 3.2 APPROACHES TO COACHING

Approach	Superior's Role
Tell	Directive Role (Do this)
Sell	Expert Role (This is the best way)
Work On Jointly	Colleague Role (Let's see what we can do)
Draw Out	Facilitator Role (What ideas do you have?)
Review and Endorse	Authorization Role (Tell me what you plan to do?)

Although the Tell and Sell approaches are time-saving, the solutions invariably come from the superior and may lead the direct report to become overly dependent on the superior to solve problems.

With the Draw Out and Review-and-Endorse approaches, the solutions are more likely to come from the direct report, especially if they are experienced or well-qualified staff.

Work On Jointly, as illustrated in Figure 3.3, is a collaborative approach with learning opportunities for the direct report on the job.

Most highly-regarded managers tend to use the joint working and drawing-out approaches, which are inductive and non-

Figure 3.3. The Joint Approach to Solving Problems

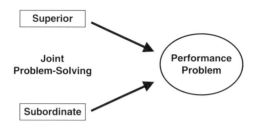

adversarial, and require tact and sensitivity in solving problems thus creating greater commitment from the direct report.

The Performance Coaching process is shown in Table 3.3.

Table 3.3 The Performance Coaching Process

Describe the performance problem
- State the expected result vs. the actual result

Find the real cause
- Reduce defensiveness
- Obtain facts from the performer
- Ascertain most probable cause
- Confirm real cause

Seek solutions
- Allow performer to suggest solutions
- Work on solution jointly
- Suggest possible solution
- Invite third-party solution

Implement solutions
- Allow performer ownership
- Obtain understanding and acceptance

Follow up on implementation
- Obtain feedback from performer
- Provide feedback

This process is logical and rational—but pure logic by itself will not necessarily solve the problem if we are dealing with human performance. In such instances, a major concern is dealing with natural defensiveness that impedes communication when something goes wrong or is below expectations. When dealing with performance issues, it helps to be descriptive rather than be evaluative. This reduces the need for the performer to be defensive.

These are the steps in the problem-solving process.

Describe the performance problem: Instead of asking why, we start with describing what. An easy, descriptive way is to state the **should** and the **actual**. This will set the tone for a joint problem-solving approach.

In our example above, the direct report *should* have set a target date. The *actual* situation was that he had not done it.

Find the real cause: To find the real cause of the problem, we need facts. Symptoms of defensiveness—such as giving opinions, making excuses, or allocating blame—will not help us to find the real cause of the problem. They will distract from the objective fact-finding.

To get facts, we need to **draw out** by clarifying and confirming, in order to understand the *what and why*. Only when we can piece the facts together will we be able to ascertain the root cause of why the performer was not meeting targets or expectations.

Seek solutions: Once the real cause is understood and accepted, it will be easier for the performer to propose solutions or contribute ideas for joint problem solving.

Usually, once a root cause is ascertained and accepted, the performer can come up with logical preventive and corrective solutions. Constructive feedback can also be used to eventually refine solutions.

Implement solutions: Implementation will be easier if there is ownership of a solution. Therefore, if the solution is not imposed as something to be complied with, but comes from the performer or is jointly developed, there will be commitment. The implementation will be more expeditious.

Follow up on implementation of solution(s): In most cases, where there is ownership of a solution, empowerment and self-control will be the best form of follow-up.

However, it is still the responsibility of the superior to monitor the implementation to give the message that performance matters and that he is interested in the current status.

While the logical problem-solving steps are a left-brain process, the soft skills of effective listening, giving credit, constructive feedback, and conflict handling are needed to make the coaching effective.

In our example, what appears on the surface to be a time-management or attitude issue may well simply be a case of the direct report not knowing how to go about the task. The time and patience required to do things properly will undoubtedly pay greater dividends than simply jumping to conclusions and to adopting a confrontational approach without taking the time to ascertain the real cause(s) of a problem.

To summarize then, the benefits of coaching include the following:

To the performer

- On-the-job learning that can be applied immediately to the problem
- Better understanding of the superior's standards and expectations
- Guidance and support from the superior

To the superior

- Opportunity to foster a closer and more trusting working relationship with the direct report
- Easier to encourage direct report to self-evaluate performance once a good working relationship is in place
- A better insight into direct report's work, and also a better understanding of the operating environment and issues affecting it
- Gain respect as a superior
- Greater probability for talent retention

(continued)

Pitfalls to avoid

- Adopting a talk-down, parent-to-child approach, instead of an adult-to-adult approach
- Using Tell and Sell more than Working On Jointly or Drawing Out
- Passing judgment about performer before finding out cause of problem
- Being in a hurry to provide solutions

Understanding natural defensiveness

It is important to recognize that the coaching process can work effectively only if natural defensiveness can be reduced. Defensiveness is a major barrier to communication. People may become defensive when their performance doesn't match expectations to protect their ego, to save face, to diminish their sense of failure or guilt, or to protect their position. These are instinctive reactions, and most people are prone to react like that. It is important to recognize symptoms of defensiveness, and know how to manage them. Symptoms of defensiveness include making excuses, allocating blame, making accusations, becoming aggressive, getting angry, showing sarcasm, going into denial, rationalizing, getting emotional, keeping quiet, pleading ignorance, showing passive acceptance, apologizing, and telling untruths.

Situations and supervisor actions that can lead to defensive behavior, together with some of the more common defensive responses, are given in Table 3.4.

Responding to defensive reactions

There are two common rules for reducing defensiveness: Avoid being defensive yourself and avoid intensifying the receiver's defensive reaction.

When a person gets defensive, and says or does something that attacks our ego, challenges us, or places the blame on us, it's natural for us to be defensive as well. This would in turn intensify the other person's defensiveness. This is clear from the following exchange:

Table 3.4 Situations and Actions That Induce Defensiveness

Situations that may induce defensiveness	Examples	Some common reactions
Being pressured for change	"I'll give you till next week to switch over to the new software completely."	"But we haven't been properly trained to use it yet." (Blame placing)
Being talked down to	"I've had more experience than you in such matters. Take it from me, it will work."	"Really? So this is a fresh approach?" (Sarcasm)
Being threatened	"Better do something about your department's high staff turnover or else heads will roll."	"It's the employees' market now. We're lucky we're not losing more than we're losing now." (Rationalizing)
Being belittled	"Any three-year-old can do that. It is a no-brainer."	"Well I guess I'm not up to the mark then. Better let someone else handle it." (Giving up)
Being accused	"The customer said that you were rude to her. Can you explain yourself?"	"Oh, was I? Which customer?" (Pleading ignorance)

Manager: *"Your report is late. It was due 10 days ago."*

Direct Report: *"You keep giving me rush jobs to do. I don't have time to work on the report."*

Manager: *"So that's your excuse? I also give others rush jobs to do, you know."*

This mutually defensive exchange could go on and on without the cause of late submission being known. The barriers to communication are being built higher and higher, making it increasingly difficult to come up with joint solutions for the real cause of the non-submission of the report.

The reason is that in defending oneself against the accusing reply, it might prompt a further defensive reaction from the other person.

One possible way around this might be to let the other person evaluate his own defensive statement by mirroring or paraphrasing his response. A mirror response is non-evaluative, and it encourages the other person to reconsider his own defensive reaction, and to correct himself if necessary. Here is an example:

> *Manager: "Your report is late. It was due 10 days ago."*
> *Direct Report: "You keep giving me rush jobs to do. I've no time to work on the report."*
> *Manager: "I'm sorry. You're saying that I keep giving you rush jobs to do, and that's why the report is late?"*

It may be that the direct report is simply trying to make excuses. On the other hand, it may well be that his reaction is true, and that the delay has been caused by the rush jobs he has been given. If so, then the next step is to find out what rush jobs were given to have caused the delay. A cool, non-confrontational, open-minded approach would be more helpful.

Handling defensiveness after it has surfaced is a corrective action. It is more productive for both parties if it can be prevented in the first place. This reduces time in resolving performance problems and leads to greater productivity.

By way of reviewing the skills covered so far—giving credit, constructive feedback, effective listening, and handling conflicts—the workshop participants at Resu Co. came up with the following suggestions on how to prevent or reduce defensiveness:

Suggestions for preventing and reducing defensiveness

- Be descriptive rather than evaluative in reviewing performance that falls below expectation. State the facts. Describe *what* is wrong rather than *who* is wrong.

- Be an expert in looking out for what is right, instead of remaining an expert at looking for what is wrong. Do that more often and the performer will tend to evaluate his own performance to improve.
- Listen more, rather than talking more.
- Avoid jumping to conclusions. Resist making assumptions about motives without first finding out more.
- State the merits of an action first, before bringing up the demerits.
- Understand and accept what is important to the other person and why it is so, before bringing up what is important to you and why it is so.
- Understand that the superior should help and guide, not assert positional power. Respect will come to you if you respect the performer.
- Pick the right time to bring up an issue. For example, the performer may not be in the best frame of mind to discuss the issue right after suffering a setback on the job or at home, or even right after a euphoric success.
- Adopt an adult-to-adult (talk-with) approach (joint problem-solving and drawing out) instead of a parent-to-child (talk-down-to) approach (tell and sell) when things go wrong.

PERFORMANCE COUNSELING—CHANGING WORK ATTITUDES

Whenever I ask workshop participants whether it is easier to coach or to counsel, the answer is almost always unanimous—counseling is more difficult.

Asked to elaborate, some people reply that changing attitudes or getting a person to want to do something is more difficult than helping a person to learn how to do it.

The difficulty is not so much in changing attitudes. The challenge lies more in the need to manage the emotions, especially when there is a threat to the performer's self-worth and self-image. If that is managed well, the willingness to change will come about more easily, as people by and large are more easily moved by emotions than by reasoning.

Three skills that are useful in managing emotions and restoring self-worth are: empathizing; paraphrasing feelings; and asking "soft" questions. These three specific skills need to be used in addition to the approaches and soft skills discussed in performance coaching.

These skills enable managers, as counselors, to preserve the self-image of performers. It is only after the performer has cooled and settled down that they can look into identifying the causes of their behavior. These skills help superiors to "listen" to the performer's feelings.

Empathizing

Empathy is the ability to feel with someone. To be able to do this, one must have experienced the same situation. Hence the saying that people are never closer than when they have the same ailments.

In some organizations, during their probation and induction periods, newly recruited supervisors have to do the same work that their frontline staff are doing. This helps them to get a feel for dealing with customers and the pressures of frontline jobs, so that they are better able to empathize with their direct reports facing difficult situations on the shop floor.

For example, a worker submits a piece of work that is below the expected standard, and his boss wants to find out more about what has gone wrong. The worker's defensive reply is: "That's the best I can do, given the tight deadlines I am working under." To cool the person down, the superior says: "I realize that working under tight deadlines is never a pleasant experience. You feel pressured." This sends a message that says "I am with you. I am in tune with how you feel about it."

Paraphrasing feelings

Paraphrasing feelings describes the listener's understanding of the performer's emotional state. Paraphrasing the direct report's feelings means letting the performer know that his feelings are understood. The sharing of feelings here would not be as intense as that in empathizing. However, it is still emotionally reassuring.

Paraphrasing feelings is used if the superior has not had the same experience as the performer and cannot empathize or feel the same way that the employee is feeling.

For example, when a frustrated staff member makes an angry comment along the lines of "The worst thing about this job is having to handle the public," his feeling could be paraphrased in this way: "It seems that you do not relish handling members of the public. Am I right?"

In empathizing or in paraphrasing feelings, we are not agreeing with the action or thinking; we are saying that we understand and accept the feelings. There should be specific follow-up clarification. After the person has cooled down, we must specify our need for expectations and standards to be met. We could say: "I understand. You feel that working under tight deadlines is very stressful. However, targets still have to be met if we are to meet customer expectations."

"Soft" questions

If empathizing and paraphrasing feelings are used to confirm our understanding of someone else's feeling, soft questions would be used to clarify the reason for having those feelings, without being provocative. A blunt "why?" can be intimidating and could sound provocative, which would serve only to heighten emotions.

In using soft questioning to clarify why, we could use *what* and *how* to find out more.

Simple examples of softening questions might include asking "What made you do that?" instead of "Why did you do that?" or "How did that happen?" instead of "Why did that happen?"

THE PERFORMANCE COUNSELING PROCESS

We can use the same logical problem-solving process in counseling to ascertain the cause or reason behind undesirable behavior, and to provide an objective basis for what is usually an emotional situation.

With counseling, there is a greater need to manage the emotional barriers to communication. We need to attend to this before proceeding to reduce normal defensiveness, to find out why the performer behaved in a certain way.

The logical problem-solving process is the same as for performance coaching. However, the use of emotion-managing skills becomes more acute. That is why most people find counseling more of an art than a straightforward skill.

The Performance Counseling process is set out in Table 3.5.

Table 3.5 The Performance Counseling Process

1. State the problem

Describe the desirable behavior and the actual undesirable behavior

2. Find the real cause

Manage emotion

Reduce defensiveness

Obtain facts not opinions from the performer

Ascertain cause or reason for the undesirable behavior

Confirm cause with paraphrasing

3. Seek solution

Empathize and draw out to assist self-reflection and willingness to
  change

Obtain understanding and acceptance of the need to change

4. Implement solution

Empathize and draw out to obtain commitment to change behavior

5. Follow up on implementation

Obtain feedback from performer

Provide positive or constructive feedback to reinforce changed behavior

In the Resu workshop, I asked the participants to apply the process to the following scenario, drawing on their own experiences of similar situations, of possible approaches to take in counseling Larry in the following scenario.

You are head of a division. Sandra, an administrative assistant who works in a department under your division, has tendered her resignation.

During her exit interview, she claims that her department head, Larry, was unreasonable and would yell at the slightest thing.

She also accuses Larry of being unpunctual himself, so she should not be picked on for being unpunctual.

This was an exercise in how to manage emotions and reduce defensiveness and the groups first came up with examples of things they should avoid saying:

- "You'll have to do something about your own unpunctuality if you want to correct your direct reports."
- "Larry, HR has given me a copy of the exit interview of one of your staff. She said that you yell at the slightest thing, and you do not show a good example yourself by coming in late often. Can you explain?"

Instead, they thought that the following lead-ins might result in a higher success rate.

- "Larry, as you know, Sandra has resigned. Good HR practice requires that we conduct an exit interview. I have the notes of the exit interview here."
- "I know that it can be exasperating when our direct reports do not do their work carefully and you have to bring it to their attention."
- "What actually happened in Sandra's case?"

(After he has given his account, the participants added, we can paraphrase understanding of his account of the reasons and proceed to the next important topic.)

- "Sandra also made one comment that may or may not be true. She said that you are often unpunctual yourself. What actually happened to make her say that?"

It was clear that the group had realized that being descriptive and using soft questions might enable Larry to reflect over what he had done, and whether he would do it differently (for example, by coming to work on time himself) in future.

To test their skills a little further, the class was then given the following case to work on. They were asked to role-play and establish the cause of the undesirable behavior.

Peter is your direct report. His work meets acceptable standards but his major drawback is the tendency to procrastinate. Recently you gave him an assignment, which he again left till the last minute. Though the work was acceptable, you feel it could have been better if he had spent more time considering all alternatives for doing it more effectively.

You feel the need to counsel Peter on performance efficiency (meeting time standards) and effectiveness (meeting quality standards). You also want him to understand that procrastination and better work quality are not synonymous.

It was interesting to observe the groups as they role-played the counseling process, using all the soft skills they had learned in overcoming Peter's initial defensiveness when he felt accused and misunderstood. Focusing on the facts, rather than on assumptions or opinions, enabled the superior to manage Peter's emotions properly. Paraphrasing his responses and empathizing with him, the superior was able to draw out the underlying reason for his procrastination. (In one particular group, Peter felt that whenever he completed his work early, he would be assigned another task to do, while others were still working on their first task. He looked upon it as punishment for being efficient. He therefore tried not to finish his tasks before deadline.)

While some might view the early completion of an assigned task as an opportunity to begin a fresh assignment, others may have different needs and may not relish another challenge. It is incumbent on the manager, therefore, to know their direct reports well, including their strengths, weaknesses, likes and dislikes.

In this case, the underlying reason for Peter's procrastination (not wanting to be "punished" with more work if he finished ahead of time) is a common phenomenon, and one that is often perceived as an attitude problem.

To this could be added three other common causes of perceived attitude problems:

1. *When performance, good or poor, is perceived as inconsequential.* This happens when good performance is taken for granted, and poor performance is ignored, in daily activities. This will be the belief fostered when appraisal ratings are bunched around "average," and everyone gets the same

bonus and same increments, as in a time-based or length-of-service type of compensation system.

2. *When there are too many impediments placed in the path of the performer.* These could include delays in decision-making; having accountability for results but having no authority to do their work; inadequate tools to do the tasks assigned; too many policies and procedures to comply with; and too much paperwork management.

3. *When people are favored for non-performance* such as currying favor, carrying tales, or doing "busy" work rather than meaningful work. This could create an unhealthy work environment that fosters negative work attitudes and divisiveness among work groups.

It is important to diagnose individual performance problems correctly, so as not to jump to the cause of problems and engage in solutions that may cause more problems. Moreover, if these problems exist in the work environment, they represent push factors, thus making talent retention difficult.[2]

To summarize then, the benefits of performance counseling include:

To the performer

- Greater awareness of self
- Greater awareness of own behavioral impact on others
- Increased acceptance by others
- Better understanding by others
- Better understanding of needed managerial changes
- Greater job satisfaction

To the superior

- Easier to counsel former peers and older direct reports
- Improved work climate
- Trusting working relationships

(*continued*)

- Respect and loyalty from direct reports
- Greater talent retention

Pitfalls to avoid

- Relying solely on logical problem-solving process to solve a problem that has emotional nuances
- Jumping to conclusions about the cause and expecting a quick fix
- Omitting to manage emotions and defensiveness before finding cause
- Being in a hurry to get to the root of the "attitude problem"
- "Telling and hard selling" instead of "drawing out"
- Taking ownership of the problem, instead of creating ownership of the problem for the direct report

It takes longer to learn how to achieve results through and with people than it does to establish performance measures and results. Performance management is critical to the success of any results-management system. As we have seen, performance management is not solely a left-brain activity. The soft skills breathe life into the results-management system, which should be viewed as a people system, and not a paper system.

While making use of all the skills, processes, and tools might take some time to settle in, after a while it becomes second nature, in much the same way that IT processes have been internalized by almost all organizations as a job aid.

It is a matter of consciously using what we have learned until we develop insights and a feel for the skills. If we tell ourselves we have no time to use these skills, we will not allocate time to practice them.

Periodic Results Reviews

As part of performance management, managers need to conduct periodic results reviews to check whether targets set are likely to be met, so that corrective actions can be taken where necessary.

These reviews are in essence diagnostic evaluations of performance, with reference to targets set. The process used is the same problem-solving process used in performance coaching and counseling.

However, we are not only looking for negative variances. Positive variances against targets set are also noted, because the causes also contribute to learning experiences.

The overall review process, as set out in Table 3.6, is the same as for problem solving, except that the positive and negative variances, as well as the causal factors, are recorded for use at annual appraisal time.

This is a very important record of performance, and should be done on at least a quarterly basis, as superiors sometimes get transferred during the year. There will then be a record for the successor to rely on for annual summative evaluations of work done during the period he was not present. Sometimes, it's the performer who gets transferred during the year, and the record of his work prior to transfer will be useful for his new superior.

There is a perception among some line managers that performance results reviews are time-consuming and perhaps excessive since there is the annual performance appraisal. This is understandable as most line managers have day-to-day operational problems to contend with. The way to have periodic results reviews accepted is to draw parallels with the company's daily, weekly, monthly, or quarterly financial, accounting or other business reports such as production reports and sales reports which also feed into the annual reports.

Individual performance results need not be formally reported as frequently as, say, sales and production. But quarterly formal updates can prove very useful at year's end for making overall annual appraisal ratings.

Where this is done less frequently—say, on a six-monthly basis, which some organizations have tried—the reviews tend to become mini-appraisals before the year-end appraisals and are looked upon as an HR administrative duty, rather than a line manager's responsibility.

It is a common mistake to regard periodic results reviews as mini-appraisals, as line managers have a responsibility to train and develop those under their charge and resolve performance

TABLE 3.6 PERIODIC RESULTS REVIEW

Process Steps	Skills to Use
1. Warm Up • State or reiterate purpose and procedure for session. • Emphasize periodic results review is joint problem solving and not a mini-appraisal.	**Clarify** **Cofirm**
2. Review Results • Subordinate reviews **high-importance specific objectives** (one at a time).	**Clarify** **Confirm**

3. Find Cause
• For **specific objectives met or exceeded**
  – Ask if any obstacles, difficulties encountered in meeting specific objectives or factors aiding achievement of objectives.
  – Ask if any new problems anticipated and explore ways to deal with them.
	Give Credit
	Draw Art
	Clarify
	Confirm

• For **specific objectives not met -**
  – Express concern.
  – Invite subordinate to identify possible causes.
  – Clarify, probe and paraphrase to get at real cause (lack of willingness/skill/knowledge).
	Clarify
	Confirm

4. Consider/Select Alternative Solutions • Invite suggestions to deal with anticipated new problems if **specific objectives are met**. Give reaction. • Invite suggestions to remove cause of problems if **specific objectives are not met**. Give reason.	**Constructive** **Feedback**
5. Implementation/Follow-up Action • Achieve understanding and agreement on follow-up action to take. • Revise specific objectives, priorities, action plans, if any.	**Clarify** **Confirm** **Handle Conflict**
6. Ending the Periodic Results Review • Summarize understanding and agreement on specific objectives. • Restate willingness to help if necessary. • Schedule next periodic results review meeting. • Provide a copy of Periodic Results Review Record for both (notes can be taken by subordinate).	**Clarify** **Confirm**

problems on the job. Many people stay in a company because they can learn from their superiors or mentors on the job.

In Figure 3.4, a gardening analogy is used to show the differences between Periodic Results Reviews and Annual Performance Appraisals.

When you plant seeds at the beginning of the year, it is like setting targets. You expect them to grow into healthy plants (results desired or expected). To enable them to do this, you have to observe them regularly, and water them when necessary. Periodically, you may need to spray on pesticides if insects and pests attack the plants (problem-solving with coaching and counseling). You add fertilizers (motivate and communicate through feedback and listening) to improve the viability of the plant.

FIGURE 3.4. PERIODIC RESULTS REVIEWS AND ANNUAL APPRAISAL COMPARED

Periodic Results Review	Annual Performance Appraisal
Seeds (Target Setting)	
• Water • Pesticide • Fertilizer (Coaching & Counseling)	• Strong plant? • Average plant? • Poor plant? (Appraisal Rating)
Role of Supervisor • Helper • Problem-Solver	**Role of Supervisor** • Judge • Decision-Maker
(Diagnostic Evaluation)	(Summative Evaluation)
Establishes Level of Difficulty Experienced	Makes Balanced Performance Rating

So the supervisor's role during the periodic results review is to nurture and help to solve problems that might prevent targets from being met. This is diagnostic evaluation.

At the end of the year, the gardener looks at the plant and concludes whether it is a healthy plant or not. The gardener is now a judge, and has to decide what to do next if the plant does not meet expectations. Try different fertilizers or pesticides? Water more/less frequently? Move the plant to a different location?

If the plant meets expectations, then the next thing to do is to enhance its growth, to enable more and better blooms or fruits with the same nurturing as before. With human beings, we reinforce good performance with rewards and nurture their talents for future roles in the organization.

Key Points to Ponder

- To manage for commitment is to win the heart and the mind of the performer.
- Performance Management is exercising managerial leadership, while Performance Measurement is part of managerial planning and control.
- Leaders turn people on by motivating, communicating, coaching and counseling.
- Effective motivators give credit when due and provide constructive feedback when performance is below expectations.
- Effective communicators listen well and handle conflicts, resulting in mutually beneficial outcomes.
- Good performance is a function of the performer's willingness to perform and ability to perform.

- Willingness to perform with commitment and passion is the heartbeat of a results-management system.
- Ability to perform requires understanding, acceptance and application.
- Performance coaching and counseling are processes for diagnosing performance problems.
- A periodic results-review session provides the organizational platform for the line manager to reinforce good performance and diagnose performance problems that persist.
- A periodic results review is not a mini-appraisal. It is assessing and reviewing work in progress, not work completed.

Endnotes

1. For a comprehensive listing of all managerial functions and activities, see Louis A. Allen's *Professional Management: new concepts and proven practices* (published by McGraw-Hill) or attend the Allen Management Program conducted by Louis Allen Inc. in various locations.
2. For more insights into diagnosing individual performance problems, I recommend *Analyzing Performance Problems* by Robert F. Mager and Peter Pipe (published by Fearon Pub. Inc.).

Chapter Four

Performance Appraisal

A summative evaluation of results achieved

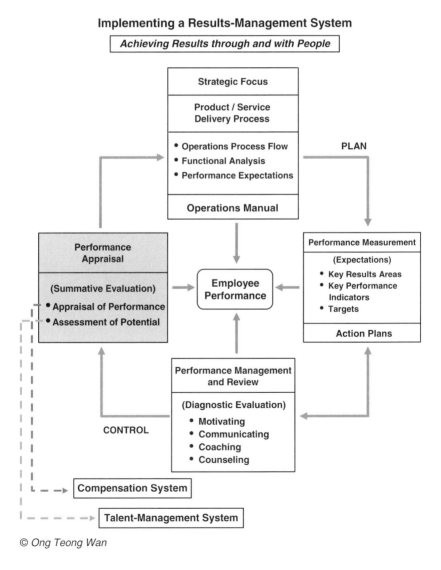

Implementing a Results-Management System

Achieving Results through and with People

Strategic Focus

Product / Service Delivery Process

- Operations Process Flow
- Functional Analysis
- Performance Expectations

PLAN

Operations Manual

Performance Appraisal

(Summative Evaluation)
- Appraisal of Performance
- Assessment of Potential

Employee Performance

Performance Measurement

(Expectations)
- Key Results Areas
- Key Performance Indicators
- Targets

Action Plans

Performance Management and Review

(Diagnostic Evaluation)
- Motivating
- Communicating
- Coaching
- Counseling

CONTROL

Compensation System

Talent-Management System

© Ong Teong Wan

93

THE PLACE OF PERFORMANCE APPRAISAL IN THE RESULTS-MANAGEMENT SYSTEM

The results-management system is not a variant of commonly used appraisal systems. It is a holistic management system to improve individual and collective productivity.

Appraisals, rewards, and talent management are important parts of the results-management system, but relative to the establishment of performance measures and managing of performance, they need less time to learn.

If measures are established well and performance is well-managed, very often performers can make their own self-appraisals objectively, comparing the results achieved against the results expected. This reduces the need for much training in interpreting descriptors in different functional contexts, conducting appraisal interviews, achieving understanding and acceptance on ratings, and handling disagreements on ratings.

The people who need to know the details of the why, what, and how of compensation and talent-management systems are the HR professionals, who have to design, develop, and maintain the systems for line managers to operate within.

The results-management system is designed for line managers to help their direct reports achieve greater individual productivity. Appraisals alone cannot achieve this. An appraisal is the summative evaluation of a year's work and the results achieved against results expected or desired. Most of the work is done at the beginning (when results expected are established) and during the year (to make sure results are on track).

Different professional groups use the words "appraisal," "assessment," and "evaluation" for different purposes and in different contexts. Since line managers are not interested in the semantic differentiation of the three words and concepts elsewhere, we would use them in the context of performance measurement and management in business organizations and not-for-profit organizations.

In the context of an organization such as Resu Co., we use the word "appraisal" as in "performance appraisal," which is to make a summative evaluation of all the actual results achieved by a performer against targets set at the beginning of the year, or (as circumstance dictates) revised during the year.

"Assessment" is usually associated with talent assessment or the assessment of potential.

The word "evaluation" as in "training evaluation" is used to measure the effectiveness of training in the acquisition of attitudes, skills, and knowledge to apply on the job to achieve results. Evaluation therefore looks at variances and their causes between the actual and the prescribed. It is part of the management-control process, which compares work in progress and the interim results achieved and work completed against targets set. It is also about determining the cause(s) of any variances.

The gist of the management-control process described below is based on the work of Louis A. Allen, a management guru whose fundamental concepts and principles on management are as valid today as when I started on my management career in the early 1970s.

THE MANAGEMENT-CONTROL PROCESS

- Establish performance measures.
- Measure actual results against expected results.
- Evaluate results achieved against results expected to ascertain causes of positive or negative variance.
- Take corrective or preventive actions to ensure results expected are met. This is a useful control device that can be used for self-regulating and external regulating.

An evaluation of periodic results reviews undertaken during the year are known as *diagnostic* evaluation. That is, it sets out to find the cause of a problem of work in progress. This is different from the end-of-year appraisal, which is stock-taking or *summative* evaluation.

MAKING A BALANCED PERFORMANCE-APPRAISAL RATING

Making a balanced performance-appraisal rating with objective measures is not merely a matter of comparing whether targets were met or not met. It is not an entirely computational exercise to be left to a computer after input from the periodic results reviews. A certain degree of judgment is needed, based on the data presented, to arrive at a final rating that will be understood and accepted.

If it is not a straightforward computation, how then does it differ from the behavior-anchored rating scales that require moderation or forced ranking to arrive at a normal distribution?

There are three levels of judgment, or decision making, about the overall evaluation of an individual's performance, as outlined in Figure 4.1, below.

FIGURE 4.1. EVALUATING INDIVIDUAL PERFORMANCE

Objective Computation of Expected vs. Actual Results

↑

Judgment based on Expected vs. Actual Results

↓

Subjective Assessment based on Behavior Observations

At a totally objective level, all that is needed is inputting the actual results achieved, comparing them against the expected results on a spreadsheet, and computing the overall rating. Little or no judgment or decision-making is required by anyone. The computer is the evaluator, not the manager or the performer.

However, during the assessment year, there could be circumstances beyond the control of the performer. These could be factors that affect results, such as epidemics, natural disasters, power outages, material shortages, lost shipments, armed conflicts, and so on. A performer may not meet his targets because of these or he may meet his targets despite them.

There could also be instances where a target is missed by a day or a single unit. These situations require refinement after the quantitative evaluation, because, to be fair, these are not normal circumstances.

Subjective judgment can be fairly accurate with experienced evaluators, just as an experienced mother will be able to diagnose a crying baby's ailment fairly correctly without going to a physician to verify with test results.

Similarly, an experienced physician can do accurate impressionistic evaluations. Along the same reasoning, judging panels for beauty contests, music contests, debates, gymnastics competitions, diving and other performance areas use experienced people to judge.

However, such ability with impressionistic evaluations is usually confined to a small percentage of managers within an organization. For the majority, without objective results on which to base judgments, the probability of error will be higher.

There is also the performer's reaction to consider, and this includes the understanding and acceptance of the evaluation, especially when the emotive element of pay is involved.

A balanced judgment—based on results and taking mitigating factors into account—reduces the probability of error in judgment. It also gives the countersigning manager a basis for endorsing or not endorsing the immediate superior's judgment or evaluation.

For this, a five-point rating scale can be used, as follows:

FE—Performance **far exceeds** expected results for the year.

EE—Performance **exceeds** expected results for the year.

FM—Performance **fully meets** expected results for the year.

PM—Performance **partially meets** expected results for the year.

NM—Performance **does not meet** expected results for the year.

With a three-point scale, the ratings would be restrictive, and there may be a tendency to add in a plus or minus in deference to the feelings of the person being appraised. This would result in a lack of consistency and rigor. A seven-point rating would give too wide a spread and may weaken the consistency among raters.

The specifications for each rating are left to individual organizations to define according to its corporate values and the performance standards desired. These ratings must be understood, accepted and applied throughout the organization for consistency of practice.

To illustrate the need for balanced judgment in refining evaluations, I presented the workshop participants at Resu Co. with the following case involving the Service Manager of a consumer-electronics distributor to consider.

The Service Manager's job was to provide after-sales service in equipment repairs and parts supply. These were his **Professional/Technical Functions** *(Key Results Areas) for which targets were set:*

- *Sales Revenue Management*
- *Customer Service*
- *Parts Inventory Control*
- *Dealer/Customer Training*

These were his **Managerial Functions** *(Key Results Areas) for which targets were set:*

- *Staff Development*
- *Human Resource Utilization*
- *Staff Communications*
- *New Appraisal System Implementation*

Using Sales Revenue from the Professional/Technical Functions area as an example, the groups were asked to arrive at a balanced performance rating on the basis of the following information.

FUNCTIONAL RESULTS AREA: SALES REVENUE

EXPECTED RESULTS PROF/TECH WORK	ACTUAL RESULTS
Sales Revenue	
1.0 To have achieved average monthly sales target of $200,000 or more.	1.0 Achieved average of $220,000 average monthly sales for the year.
1.1 At least 50 percent of the revenue from sale of parts, and 50 percent from labor charges.	1.1 60 percent of revenue from sale of parts. 40 percent from labor charges.

(Continued)

1.2	All maintenance contracts are renewed one week before expiry.	1.2	Out of 50 maintenance contracts, eight were renewed after one week of expiry.
			10 did not renew.
			The rest renewed on time.
1.3	Re-dos on repairs are to be less than 5 percent of all jobs handled.	1.3	Re-dos on repairs of jobs handled for the year came in at 6 percent.

The groups discussed this in their groups. These were their evaluations:

FUNCTIONAL RESULTS AREA: SALES REVENUE

Evaluators	1.0	1.1	1.2	1.3	Overall Result
Engineering	A	A	B	B	O
Production	A	A	FB	B	B
Sales and Marketing	FA	FA	B	FB	A
Facilities	A	A	B	B	O
Finance	FA	FA	FB	B	A
Human Resources	FA	A	B	FB	O

Key	
FA = Far Above Target	B = Below Target
A = Above Target	FB = Far Below Target
O = On Target	

From the same set of facts the groups produced quite different final ratings. For the Engineering Group it was "a straightforward matter of two Above Targets and two Below Targets. On balance, the overall result is On Target."

For the Production Group, however, "the renewal of maintenance contracts is very important. That's why we rated that performance as Far Below Target. As for re-dos, it is only one percent off target, and we rated it Below Target, giving an overall rating of Below Target.''

The Sales and Marketing Group's reasoning for their rating for an area within their area of concern and expertise was as follows: "We gave Target 1.0 a Far Above Target rating, as it's very difficult to average $200,000 sales per month under current economic conditions. As for achieving 10 percent more in parts sales, we rated it Far Above too, because most people prefer to go elsewhere for non-original parts, which are less costly. It is actually a hard target to achieve and to exceed it is really commendable. As for maintenance contracts, we agree with the Engineers that it is Below Target. As for re-dos, we think this has great impact on customer perception and may affect our future product sales. Therefore, we rated it Far Below Target. The overall rating is sort of averaged out to Above Target."

The Facilities Group reported that, like the Engineering Group, they had done the ratings in a straightforward and logical manner, thus arriving at the same conclusion.

The Finance Group explained that they agreed with the Sales and Marketing group's rating for monthly sales and sale of parts. However, they rated renewal of maintenance contracts as Far Below Target because this had long-term impact on future revenue. Also, having heard the Sales and Marketing group discussing the impact of re-dos on customer perception, they revised their rating from Below Target to Far Below Target, giving them an overall rating that was still Above Target.

The HR Group agreed that exceeding the average monthly sales revenue in the current economic climate deserved be rated Far Above Target. They rated sale of parts Above Target, and gave a Below Target rating to the renewal of maintenance contracts, which they said "should be a routine process for us to stay in business, as most of the other services are part of our warranty commitments." Taking into consideration the "inconveniences and irritations" caused to customers by re-dos, they rated this factor Far Below Target. This made their overall rating On Target.

From all of this it is clear that while some managers will take the results at face value and arrive at the overall results accordingly, others may consider the level of importance of the targets, or the difficulty entailed in achieving them.

We must not forget the implications of these evaluation considerations and ratings on the performer, especially if they affect bonuses and increments when these results are used for deciding compensation and rewards. That being the case, should we take into account the relative importance and the difficulty level of each target, besides looking at Efficiency (Quantity and Time) and Effectiveness (Quality, Cost, and Human Impact or Reaction)? Possible objections to doing so might be that this would make the process more subjective and might be seen as giving excuses for not achieving the targets. Is it not the case, as Eugene from the Engineering Group asserted in the discussion that followed, that "results are results, no matter what the causes are"?

When an organization sets its targets at the beginning of the year it makes them challenging and achievable in the context of the conditions that prevail then. The level of difficulty should only be considered perhaps when conditions change to make it easier or more challenging. It is this factor that underscores the value of periodic results reviews, in that they provide a better idea of what is happening at ground level and in the market place during the year. The information they provide throws light on those who have performed well under difficult circumstances, as well as those who have not met their targets. Talented performers can be recognized and rewarded, making it more likely that the organization will retain their talents.

Conversely, there may be others who exceed their targets but only because conditions became less challenging than when the targets were set. For example, a competitor closes down and you are the only supplier in that location. Or political conditions may change to make things easier, as when during the Gulf War former colleagues in a dry-cell battery company found that they did not have to leave their desks to go the Middle East to sell, as the orders just kept pouring in. In such situations, the level of difficulty becomes lower and this too should be taken into account during evaluation, so that there is fairness and no unnecessary envy.

Again the value of periodic results reviews is apparent: they help us to understand how ongoing conditions are affecting targets, whether they are being met, not met, or exceeded, and the difficulties that have to be overcome. They also serve as recognition of effort put in.

I then listed on the flipchart the usefulness of the periodic results reviews in helping appraisers to arrive at balanced performance ratings:

Usefulness of Periodic Results Reviews
Enable the superior to have a good feel of what is on the ground operationally and in the market place.
Make it easier to decide on a balanced summative evaluation of a direct report's performance later.
Help to develop a closer working relationship between superior and direct report.
Minimize surprises at year-end performance appraisal.
Provide a record of results and factors in case of transfers during the year.

The Periodic Results Review Record for four quarters from our example above might look as shown in Figure 4.2. Such records would be used to provide a summary of the whole year's results.

From all of this, we can conclude that the following factors must be considered if we are to make a balanced performance-appraisal rating:

- Efficiency (quantity and time)
- Effectiveness (quality, cost, and human impact or reaction)
- Level of importance (weighting for targets within a functional results area)
- Level of difficulty (unexpected conditions arising during the year that make a target easy or difficult to achieve)
- The relative weighting between professional/technical work and management work (for a managerial position)

The level of difficulty (high, medium, or low) can only be ascertained over the year, depending on conditions affecting the achievement of the targets.

It is vital that the performer understands what the superior's expectations are and where the areas of focus should be. These have to be understood and agreed on when targets are set at the beginning of the year.

Considering level of importance and level of difficulty also serves another purpose. Some targets cannot be exceeded, such as achieving zero accidents. If a plant is able to achieve zero accidents after a defined period of operation, then this target is very well achieved, and should be rated Far Exceeds, taking into account the level of importance and level of difficulty.

Let's say the relative weighting between professional/technical work and managerial work for the Service Manager is 50/50, and these are the following overall results for each results area.

Results Areas	Overall Results		
Sales Revenue	Above Target	Above Target	Above Target
Customer Service	Above Target	On Target	On Target
Parts Inventory Control	Above Target	On Target	On Target
Dealer/Customer Training	On Target	On Target	On Target
Staff Development	On Target	Above Target	On Target
Human Resource Utilization	On Target	On Target	On Target
Staff Communications	On Target	On Target	On Target
Implement New Appraisal System	On Target	On Target	On Target
Overall Performance Rating	**X ?**	**Y ?**	**Z ?**

How do we arrive at the overall performance rating in this case? Should we accord the Service Manager an overall performance rating of Exceeds Expected Results or Fully Meets Targets? I

FIGURE 4.2. PERIODIC RESULTS REVIEW RECORD

Periodic Results Review Record						Subordinate's Copy	
Specific Objectives (S.O.) Q = Quarter A = Above S.O. O = Met S.O. B = Below S.O.	Action Plan #	Q	Results Review A	O	B	Actual Performance - Performance standards - S.O. achieved achieved - Follow-up actions - Causes of variance	L O D
Prof/Tech Work 1.0 Sales Revenue (Impt - High) To have achieved average monthly sales target of $200,000 or more		1			*	1.0 Average mthly sales was $190,000 Post holiday period	
					*	1.1 40 percent from parts and 40 percent from labor	
				*		1.2 All maintenance contracts renewed on schedule	
					*	1.3 6 percent of re-dos	
Performance Standards 1.1 At least 50 percent of the revenue from sale of parts and 50 percent from labour charges 1.2 All maintenance contracts are renewed one week before expiry		2			*	1.0 Average mthly sales was $195,000	D3
				*		1.1 50 percent from parts and 50 percent from labor	
					*	1.2 5 maintenance contracts for renewal did not reach customer 2 wks overdue – Dispatch oversight	
					*	1.3 7 percent of re-dos	

	3	*	*			D2
1.3 Re-dos on repairs are less than 5 percent of all jobs handled						D2
1.0 Average mthly sales was $235,000					*	
1.1 70 percent from parts and rest from labor						
1.2 3 maintenance contracts for renewal not sent by clerk till due date - her oversight due to heavy workload			*			D2
1.3 8 percent re-dos due to increasing workload					*	
1.0 Average mthly sales was $260,000	4	*				
1.1 80 percent on parts. The rest from labor		*				
1.2 All maintenance contracts renewed on time 10 non-renewals			*			
1.3 11 percent re-dos. Year-end volume					*	D2

Level of Difficulty (LOD)		Rating
Extremely Difficult	(High)	D3
Difficult	(Medium)	D2
Less Difficult	(Low)	D1

Level of Importance (LOI)		Rating
Extremely Important	(High)	Impt 3
Important	(Medium)	Impt 2
Less Important	(Low)	Impt 1

put these questions to the workshop participants. The following is a summary of their deliberations.

In Eugene's view: "If we were to use points and ranges to depict each rating level, then whether there are three results areas above target or just one above target, with the rest on target, the overall rating will be Exceeds Expected Results. Of course, we can adjust our point ranges to reflect the type of performance standards and corporate values that we cherish, as you said earlier on. Using an impressionistic evaluation, I would also rate Exceeds Expected Results for Z, except that the contrast with X may appear stark and unfair."

Sally added: "The results would be different if you had specified Sales Revenue and Customer Service or Staff Communications as being more important than the others. I suppose if we want to accord Z the same rating as X and Y, we could add in another fine-tuning factor, maybe Teamwork, to reflect our corporate values. If Z has displayed great teamwork, then we can comfortably rate that as Exceeds Expected Results. This is one way of building teamwork into the work culture, as part of our value system. Of course measures have to be established for teamwork too so that there is measurability."

All of these suggestions can be used as guiding concepts to establish an evaluation system that is applicable throughout the company for consistency and fairness. They can incorporate the organization's corporate values, the expectations of each superior, the performance standards required within each department, and so on.

But there has to be a basic framework to use these factors on, so that there is at least perceived reliability and validity in the summative evaluations. The steering committee set up to implement the results-management system will need to establish the guidelines and framework for the evaluation system to capture the organization's values.

Rather than simply appraising Professional/Technical and Managerial Performance, a comprehensive performance appraisal system could include the upholding of the organization's values such as teamwork and also competencies gained during the year.

It could be in three parts:

Part 1: Appraisal of past contributions to the organization's previous year's results through the Managerial/Professional and Technical key result areas

Part 2: Appraisal of present adherence to Corporate Values in key results areas to strengthen the organization

Part 3: Appraisal of Competency Development in key results areas to ensure the organization can compete better in the future

The results could be used to compensate accordingly, such as:

Part 1: To determine how to award **Variable Bonuses**

Part 2: To determine how to award **Base Pay Increments**

Part 3: To determine how to award **Special Incentives**

Annual Performance-Appraisal Discussion

The steps involved in an annual performance-appraisal discussion are set out in Figure 4.3.

Using this process does not guarantee that the discussion will be contention-free, especially when monetary rewards are related to the appraisal rating. However, because the system is results-based, it makes it possible for the performer to do a self-appraisal that reduces the need for defensiveness. As mentioned in the chapters on Performance Measurement and Performance Management, ownership of the results and acceptance of accountability as though the performer were conducting a business-within-a business will increase the likelihood of a business-like conduct of this sensitive phase in results management.

Figure 4.3. Annual Performance Appraisal

Process Steps	Skills
Preparation • Review performance records • Superior and subordinate to complete performance ratings separately • Obtain understanding and agreement with countersigning officer • Arrange meeting • Anticipate difficulties	*Summative Evaluation*

(Continued)

Warm-Up • Put employee at ease • Create relaxed atmosphere • Get employee involved early in the interview	*Conflict Handling*
Review Performance • Performer shares self-appraisal results and rating • Superior shares appraisal rating of Subordinate • Areas of divergence are discussed and resolved, if any • Understanding and acceptance of overall performance rating concluded	*Draw Out Clarify Confirm*
Follow-Up Action ☞ Discuss performance improvement plan ☞ Establish needs for ensuing year	*Conflict Handling Clarify Confirm*
Closing ☞ Summarise discussion ☞ Arrange discussion on career directions	*Constructive Feedback Clarify Confirm*

Key Points to Ponder

• Performance appraising is only one aspect of a results-management system.

• We **appraise** performance, **assess** potential, and **evaluate** results achieved against results expected to ascertain causal factors for variances.

(*continued*)

- Evaluating results for work in progress is diagnostic evaluation done during periodic results reviews.

- Evaluating results for work completed is summative evaluations which is done at the end of a year in the form of a performance appraisal.

- There is an element of informed judgment involved in making balanced appraisal ratings, and making such ratings is not a mechanical or computerized process.

- A balanced performance appraisal takes into account not only results achieved, but also the level of difficulty experienced in achieving them.

- Some key results areas are more critical than others and carry greater weight so that performers know what to focus on.

- A comprehensive appraisal system should take into account:

  - appraisal of **past** contributions;

  - appraisal of **present** adherence to corporate values; and

  - appraisal of competency development for the **future** viability of the enterprise.

Chapter Five

COMPENSATION SYSTEM

Paying for the job. Paying market rates. Paying for performance

Implementing a Results-Management System

Achieving Results through and with People

	Strategic Focus	
	Product / Service Delivery Process	
	• Operations Process Flow • Functional Analysis • Performance Expectations	**PLAN**
	Operations Manual	

Performance Appraisal

(Summative Evaluation)
• Appraisal of Performance
• Assessment of Potential

Employee Performance

Performance Measurement

(Expectations)
• Key Results Areas
• Key Performance Indicators
• Targets

Action Plans

Performance Management and Review

(Diagnostic Evaluation)
• Motivating
• Communicating
• Coaching
• Counseling

CONTROL

Compensation System

Talent-Management System

© Ong Teong Wan

At the next training session, on compensation, I told the Resu group about a friend of mine whose company was swamped with orders just as it was about to close down for a two-week vacation. Desperate to fulfill these orders, rather than using temps who would not be familiar with the business operations, the company offered employees of all levels two weeks' pay in lieu of leave to multi-task. I asked the participants for their views on whether this offer would motivate people and, if so, which members of staff would be likely to respond to the offer.

The responses were varied. The Facilities Group, for example, felt that the managerial group would be unlikely to take up the offer, but would "go on vacation, especially if it is during the school holidays. The non-managerial staff would take the pay and carry on working because they need the money more."

The Sales Group thought that the majority would carry on working because "Two weeks' pay can be quite substantial, whatever the category of employees."

The Production Group thought that some might take one week's vacation and one week's pay, if they have not had a vacation with their families before this, assuming this was permissible.

The Finance Group had a quite different view: "We feel managers should understand the importance of clearing the build up of orders and carry on working. Non-managers may or may not take the leave, depending on their financial needs but the majority are likely to take the pay."

The HR Group summarized the different viewpoints for me. "It is clear," they said, "that different people have different value sets. We cannot assume that non-managers need more money and therefore they will take the pay in lieu. Likewise, we cannot assume managers will forgo their pay because they are paid more. We therefore cannot assume that pay is the main motivator for all people."

Following this discussion, I told them what actually happened. Much to the surprise of those present, the majority of the company's managerial staff took pay in lieu of leave and the majority of the non-managerial staff took leave in lieu of pay. The reason for this was that the non-managerial group had already clocked up a great deal of overtime and wanted a break to be with their families.

Contrary to what many believe, money isn't everything and neither is it the mother of all motivators.

There are many ways of rewarding people for good performance. Increasing base pay is the obvious example, but awarding variable bonuses or offering one-off monetary incentives can motivate just as well. In fact, I recall reading a study done some years back that showed that the motivational value of a salary increment, for whatever reason, normally does not last more than two weeks.

To give a business perspective to what is often considered an HR concern, I sought the groups' views on compensation as a business enabler by posing the following questions as it pertained to their company:

- What percentage of your sales revenue is expended on employee payroll—high, moderate, or low?
- How effectively has the payroll been used to benefit the company and the employees for the long-term viability of the company?

These were the consolidated answers from the groups:
Percentage of Payroll Costs to Sales Revenue:
High, edging towards 40 percent.
Effectiveness of Payroll:
Ineffective: Perception is that Sales and Marketing jobs are paid more than Admin Support and Production.
Ineffective: Bulk of payroll goes to chiefs; less goes to the warriors.
Ineffective: Overtime costs have become permanent features.
Effective: Staff turnover figures are still below industry average.
Effective: We are paying competitively at market rates. Key managerial vacancies are filled within requisition period.
Effective: No one is exceeding established salary ranges.

As these responses indicate, views on such matters are varied and dependent on the criteria adopted for determining what constitutes effective or ineffective use of payroll to attract, motivate, and retain talent for greater productivity.

Finance people generally agree that for greater productivity, fixed costs must be controlled to make room for more variable costs. Basic pay is compounded over the years, which means that managements need to find a balance between basic pay increases and variable bonuses as a compensation package—which makes the linkage to the results-management system more meaningful.

Line managers will find it useful to have a macro view of compensation systems within which the people under their charge are compensated or rewarded and how these relates to the results-management system.

The three key components of a sound compensation system are as follows:

Paying for the job: Establishing internal equity among jobs by evaluating their relative worth.

Paying market rates: Maintaining the external competitiveness of the company's jobs in the job market.

Paying for performance: Paying according to results achieved.

PAYING FOR THE JOB: ESTABLISHING INTERNAL EQUITY

This is the process by which jobs within the organization are compared to determine their relative worth to the organization.

How jobs are evaluated

There are two general approaches to job evaluation—the quantified and unquantified approaches.

The quantified approach uses factors common to jobs, and assigns point values to the factors for each job. The point values are then added up for all the factors, and ranges of points are established for job gradings.

The unquantified approach looks at whole jobs based on job descriptions. It then ranks them, categorizes them, or classifies them into job groups and grades.

Job factors include professional and technical and/or managerial knowledge and skills that are required to do the job. The competency levels required, as well as the degree and magnitude of accountability for results, are taken into consideration.

Also included for evaluation is the effort required to perform the job, or the level of difficulty inherent in the job. This is different from the level of difficulty experienced (while trying to accomplish targets) as a result of unforeseen circumstances or conditions outside the control of the performer.

Other factors could include working conditions—the amount of problem solving required, or environmental factors such as dust, noise, heat, cold, and danger, and so on. Within these main factors there could be sub-factors. For example, for problem solving, we could be looking at the level of analytical or creative thinking required.

The jobs are evaluated factor by factor and awarded point values. Benchmark jobs are evaluated first, followed by other special jobs within the organization. These special jobs are evaluated using the factors in the benchmark jobs as a basis for comparison.

Benchmark jobs are representative, universal, or commonly occurring jobs that can be found in many organizations. Benchmark jobholders could include Sales Managers, Engineers, Production Supervisors, Accountants, IT Analysts, HR Managers, and so on. However, jobs should be evaluated based on the job content, responsibility, authority level and accountability level, rather than simply on job title.

Evaluations are normally done by a committee of senior management personnel trained in the chosen evaluation system, with staff specialists included. The senior management staff are usually drawn from key functions such as Sales, Production, Engineering, IT, or HR.

However, no system is perfect. What we aspire to are acceptable perceptions of validity and reliability of evaluation. The evaluations are reviewed regularly, especially when the organization is being restructured and job functions are merged or split.

Establishing salary ranges

After the evaluations are done, jobs of the "same worth" are grouped into the same job grades, each of which will have a salary range assigned to it. Each salary grade will have a minimum base pay, a mid-point base pay, and a maximum base pay.

The mid-point value of a job is taken to be the "going rate," or market rate, for that job. It indicates what the employee should be paid if he is performing a "full job."

The mid-point pay is not to be confused with an employee's actual performance. It does not imply average performance. Any pay below the mid-point, therefore, indicates that the employee is not yet performing the "full job" for which he has been employed. A new employee is not normally placed on the mid-point base pay, unless he has a wealth of experience and can undertake the "full job" immediately upon joining the organization.

The maximum for each range is often 20 percent above the mid-point, and the minimum is often 20 percent below the mid-point. This means that there is a 50 percent difference between the minimum and the maximum, as illustrated in Table 5.1 below.

Given acceptable performance and normal increments, a new engineer in a stable job market joining the organization at the minimum of the range at $2,000 would normally reach the mid-point salary in about four years and the maximum in about eight years, assuming moderate increments and that there are no drastic labor-market changes, promotions, or salary re-structuring. Fast-track, top performers would expect to reach the maximum in a shorter time, of course. In practice, when there is a shortage of a particular job type, most job-holders expect to be promoted or upgraded before they reach the mid-point.

TABLE 5.1. SAMPLE SALARY RANGES

Job Title	Job Grade	Salary Range		
		Minimum	Mid-Point	Maximum
Manager X	1	2,400	3,000	3,600
Manager Y	1			
Manager Z	1			
Engineer	2	2,000	2,500	3,000
Accountant	2			
Systems Analyst	2			

Usually those employed at the minimum of the range have minimum experience and basic qualifications for the job, and they gain experience as they progress in the job. When an acceptable performer reaches the maximum in his salary range he might expect to be promoted to the next salary grade. If he is not, he remains at the maximum until the mid-point moves with the market. Sometimes, specific expertise is scarce. It is then necessary to accommodate a particular individual by paying him or her above the maximum, and this is referred to as a "red circled" rate, personal to the incumbent.

Conversely, sometimes a person could be paid below the minimum. This might happen where a new recruit from another organization might be asked to undergo a period of probation while he proves that he can perform to the required level. This lower, "green circled" rate, however, should be regarded as a temporary measure.

Thus, salary ranges are necessary to:

- provide a basis for comparing relative monetary values of jobs;
- gauge a performer's length of service in a certain position;
- spot talent that has been recognized by their position in the salary range;
- pay attention to high performers;
- gauge the suitability of under-performers;
- ascertain the competitiveness of the pay structure relative to the market; and
- track adherence to salary policy during high and low demand for a particular job type.

An organization's salary ranges reflect its salary policy. The salary policy is an open declaration of how the organization wants to pay or reward its employees. Having a stated policy in the employee handbook enhances the credibility of the compensation system, as it makes it transparent, even though personal pay is a private and confidential matter. Most salary policies will state pay equity, making clear the relative values of jobs to the organization as reflected in the salary grades and ranges.

They will also state how competitive the organization intends to be—whether consistently above the market, matching the market, or slightly below the market.

They may also assert whether the organization wants to pay for performance or for seniority. If they pay for seniority or length of service, the salary ranges will be very long, as observed in some collective agreements in the past.

In salary policies, there could also be a statement about the non-discriminatory nature of the pay system in tandem with the organization's hiring policies. There will be a declaration about equal pay for equal work and paying for performance, regardless of age, gender, race, nationality, language, or creed.

The basic purpose of every organization's compensation system is to attract and retain competent people. Having done that, the next thing is to motivate them for greater productivity, as part of a results-management system.

PAYING MARKET RATES: MAINTAINING EXTERNAL COMPETITIVENESS

Even though salary administration deals with numbers and is quantitative in nature, to the individual employee, salaries will always remain emotive issues. How often have you heard comments such as "I don't think people in our department are fairly paid, compared to other firms;" "My university classmate, performing the same function in ABC Co., is paid so much more than me;" "I thought I performed well last year, and yet I received only an X percent merit increase;" "I've been here 10 years but that newcomer is getting about the same pay as me;" or "admin people are more valued than operations people"?

Such complaints and laments are commonplace and employees will always compare salary according to their notion of fairness. These comparisons will be more acute if they are not aware of how a sound compensation system is arrived at. If an employee feels unjustly compensated, it will be a dormant push factor, and retention will be more challenging, especially if there are pull factors as well.

Ensuring external competitiveness is one way for an organization to verify employees' claims by comparing what it does with what is done by other organizations or the market in general. Part of this process is to conduct salary surveys.

Conducting salary surveys

Salary surveys are a common mode of collecting data to establish market competitiveness and salary trends. These trends are relative to supply and demand for talent, as well as macro-economic conditions.

Companies can obtain competitiveness data by conducting their own survey, or participating in surveys by external agencies, organizations or special-interest groups.

Whichever mode of data collection is used, how useful the data is depends on the validity and reliability of what is collected and collated. Relevance and consistency of the salary data are key considerations in salary surveys.

Factors to take into account when participating in, initiating, or organizing a salary survey include: characteristics of respondents such as relevance of data sources (comparing like with like with respect to business type, industry type, age of the company, and workforce); benchmark positions available; sample size; and components of the overall compensation package.

Determining the statistical techniques used to establish the market trends, the industry or market rates, and the organization's position relative to them will usually be the responsibility of the survey agencies involved.

For each year, however, the company will have to decide on a salary policy line, the short-term annual objective against which the salary administration will be done. The relative position of that salary line (see Figure 5.1) vis-à-vis the market is determined by business conditions, the company's financial health, and its ability to pay for that year.

The rationale for the salary policy line adopted for the year will then be communicated to management for understanding and acceptance before being used to determine the mid-point

FIGURE 5.1. ESTABLISHING THE SALARY POLICY LINE

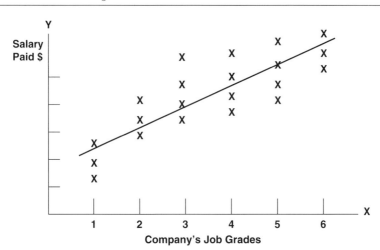

of the salary ranges, which could be above, equal to, or below the market average. Once the mid-point is adjusted in accordance with the annual salary policy line, the whole salary range will move.

It is worth reiterating here that paying the highest salaries does not necessarily produce exemplary commitment. Salaries are not motivators per se. They are reinforcers for good performance and inducers for weak performance. Salaries complement sound performance management.

PAYING FOR PERFORMANCE: ENSURING PRODUCTIVITY

"What performance should we be paying for?" I asked the workshop participants. This is what they came up with:

- *Pay for results, not for activities*—the distinction here is between "productive" work and "busy" work. The organization should pay for performance, not simply for "busyness." These results should not be achieved to the detriment of others in the organization.

- *Pay for intended outcomes, not for perverted outcomes*—in the case of the Sales team this had meant incorporating collections (poor collections were, as we saw in an earlier chapter, its own ''perverted outcomes'') as a key result area for paying commissions.

- *Pay more variable bonus on results and less on length of service*—paying variable bonuses based on company and individual results will not burden the company with high fixed base-pay costs in the near and long term. In some countries, an employer may need to contribute a certain percentage of base pay to retirement funds or medical funds. Benefits such as loans, un-utilized paid leave, medical insurance premiums, and overtime are also computed against an employee's base pay, making it necessary to moderate base pay increases. These, plus cost-of-living increases and performance-based merit increments, often lead to a need to increase prices of products and services and, ultimately, to loss of business as customers go elsewhere.

- Base pay and variable bonuses need to be balanced against other factors such as work environment, superior–direct report relationships, inter-functional working relationships, company policy on work-life balance, and the balance between cash compensation and benefits/welfare compensation, all of which have an impact on the company's ability to retain its staff.

- *Pay for adherence to corporate values and for willingness to improve skills and knowledge*—a company's values, and the development of skills and knowledge, are part of its intellectual capital, its inner strength. They must be cultivated and recognized by being built in to the company's pay-for-performance policy. Developing competencies through off-site or on-the-job training and experience such as multi-tasking is more cost-effective than hiring temps who are not steeped in the culture of the company. Staff who display such competencies need to be rewarded. This ties in with both of the following points, too.

- Pay for innovations and improvements made.

- Pay for team spirit and teamwork.

All of these components can become fixed or variable increments to the base pay. But rewarding the performer also has to take the long-term impact on the business into consideration.

Between them, the participants drew up the following outline of their proposed reward system:

Performance Appraisal	Forms of Reward to Consider
Managerial/Professional/ Technical results for the period past	Variable Bonus: Organizational level for all Individual level on merit
Adherence to corporate values	Base-pay increment
Competency development applied on the job	Variable one-off incentive

Management, with advice from the salary administrators, can decide on the percentage of the salary budget to allocate to each component. The allocations can be guided by the organization's business performance, labor-market conditions, industry trends, and the prevailing economic conditions.

A cost-of-living allowance can be added as a separate component to add to the base pay but that would have the effect of inflating base salaries again.

Paying for performance vis-à-vis base pay position in salary range

Consider the following scenario:

A company has two Engineers, A and B. Engineer A is new and B is more senior.

Engineer A's base pay is $2,500, while Engineer B's is $3,500. Both have the same appraisal rating—Exceeds Expected—for the results they achieved for targets. Such a rating commands a bonus of two months' pay.

Taking into account the difference in their base pay, is the bonus fair to Engineer A?

Few would dispute that this decision is fair, even though the absolute amounts are different for the same performance rating.

People generally accept variable bonuses based on base pay. Furthermore, the targets for the more senior engineer may have been more challenging than those for the new engineer.

But what about annual merit increments, which are also based on base pay? Should the two engineers receive the same percentage salary increase? The general response to this from within the group was that Engineer A should receive a higher percentage increase. Otherwise, he would always lag behind Engineer B, and the focus should be on performance rather than length of service.

In such circumstances, companies should have some kind of guide (similar to that shown in Table 5.2) to take account of this need. This could then be adjusted annually, depending on survey results and the selected salary policy for the year.

TABLE 5.2. SAMPLE SALARY-INCREASE GUIDE

Performance Rating	Position in Salary Range		
	80%	*100%*	*120%*
Far Exceeds	15%	9%	5%
Exceeds Expected	13%	7%	3%
Fully Meets	10%	5%	–
Partially Meets	5%	3%	–
Does Not Meet	–	–	–

Even though such matters usually fall within the general responsibilities of the HR department, all line managers must at least be able to explain the rationale behind the company's salary ranges. The compensation system has to support the company's performance measurement, management, and appraisal systems. All systems and sub-systems must operate effectively to ensure that the whole organization is not dysfunctional.

Having a consistent compensation system also enables staff to be transferred between affiliate companies without causing chaos, confusion and possible discontent borne of envy or perceptions of unfairness.

Every line manager also has a responsibility to see that their people are compensated properly and fairly, to reduce de-motivating comparisons and misperceptions.

Key Points to Ponder

- Monetary rewards can be a good motivator but they are not the sole motivator.
- The line manager, while desiring to reward his direct reports for good performance, needs to understand the big picture of the compensation system, to better appreciate his role in management.
- A comprehensive compensation system encompasses paying for the job, paying market rates, and paying for performance.
- Embedding monetary rewards into base pay is increasing fixed costs that compound over time, and this has to be borne by the organization into the future.
- There are many ways of providing variable monetary rewards to reinforce good performance and increase productivity, and yet not subject the organization to long-term overheads.
- Paying for performance does not mean paying only for results achieved for the year. It also incorporates areas outside current job duties, including rewarding employees who adhere to the organization's core values or who obtain competencies for enhancing its productivity and long-term competitiveness.

CHAPTER SIX

TALENT-MANAGEMENT SYSTEM

Placing the right talent in the right place at the right time

Implementing a Results-Management System

Achieving Results through and with People

Strategic Focus

Product / Service Delivery Process

- Operations Process Flow
- Functional Analysis
- Performance Expectations

Operations Manual

PLAN

Performance Measurement

(Expectations)
- Key Results Areas
- Key Performance Indicators
- Targets

Action Plans

Performance Appraisal

(Summative Evaluation)
- Appraisal of Performance
- Assessment of Potential

Employee Performance

Performance Management and Review

(Diagnostic Evaluation)
- Motivating
- Communicating
- Coaching
- Counseling

CONTROL

Compensation System

Talent-Management System

© Ong Teong Wan

Performance appraisal is, as we have seen, a summative evaluation of the results achieved by the performer at the end of the year. The compensation system recognizes, rewards and reinforces good performance.

An organization needs to achieve results consistently to guarantee its future existence. To do so, it needs to identify, attract, develop, retain, and renew talent. The talent-management system is designed to do of all this. To do it well, it has to serve the needs of both the individual performer and the organization.

The assessment of potential within the organization begins this process. Part of the data for the assessment of potential is gleaned from how the individual has performed under varying circumstances, situations and challenges during the year to achieve (or fail to achieve) the expected results. It is a real-life assessment center, with observations being made on the job.

There are a number of issues that need to be considered when implementing a talent-management system. These include:

- What exactly do we mean by "talent" and "talent management"?
- How is talent management different from career/succession planning?
- In talent management, are we thinking of the top echelon of high potential and star employees, or are we thinking of all the employees in an organization?
- Talent management is a strategic issue. How do we get line managers to put it into operation?
- With regionalization, globalization, greater mobility of competent workers, and the emphasis on paying for performance rather than loyalty, will talent management be a worthwhile exercise?
- How do we go about identifying, developing, retaining, and renewing talent?

WHAT DO WE MEAN BY "TALENT" AND "TALENT MANAGEMENT"?

The common understanding of "talent" is that it refers to special individual endowments with regard to creative, artistic, or sporting endeavors. We often think of someone having a gift, a knack or an aptitude for mastering a skill, usually in music, art, literature, a sport, acting, and the like.

Economic connotations of talent have extended to many other fields of human endeavor such as IT, quantitative disciplines, languages, finance, law, medicine, management and other areas of knowledge and their applications.

Indeed, talent goes beyond intuitive skills and insight to include a person's attributes or traits, which might be analytical ability, business acumen, resourcefulness, creativity, single-mindedness, charisma, introversion, extroversion, team-spiritedness, pragmatism, openness, a trusting nature, being meticulous, being careful, natural leadership and any other trait that can contribute to positive results relevant to a specific environment.

In short:

Talent = acquired skills and knowledge + attributes (including aptitude)

Talent management in an organizational setting is providing the conditions for the talent-owners within an organization to contribute significantly to the organization's results. Some advocates describe talent management as ''optimizing the talent pool.''

Talent management has to do with providing a **conducive work environment** for **talent** to bloom so as to ensure **sustainable results**.

A talent-management system provides the framework, the processes, the organizational structures, the people-management policies and the procedures for talent to be enhanced and used effectively. It includes career development and succession planning.

This chapter deals with issues and challenges connected with identifying, sourcing, developing, retaining and renewing talent for organizations of all types.

You may recall the equation—Performance = Willingness + Ability (Talent)—that we discussed in an earlier chapter. Willingness to perform is an essential part of achieving performance results. Some people may be talented, but they may have to be induced or motivated to contribute to results.

Talent management seeks to provide an environment in which people will want to readily commit their talents to achieve great results themselves or through and with others.

Performance management seeks to motivate people at all levels to be willing and be committed to use their skills and knowledge to produce great results within their capabilities.

Talent management is not just about the movers and shakers, the well-trained, well-educated, high-potential individuals within the organization. For such individuals to thrive there has to be a solid support team of acceptable performers with acceptable potential (sometimes referred to as "solid citizens"). There is also talent in them but in a different shade.

Current thinking is more in terms of human-capital development and management, and treating it as being as important as financial capital management, with a long-term perspective.

Like all forms of assets, some groups of human capital can generate more added value than others, but they all create value as assets of the organization.

Figure 6.1 broadly outlines a typical distribution of talent in a sizeable organization.

FIGURE 6.1. THE DISTRIBUTION OF TALENT WITHIN AN ORGANIZATION

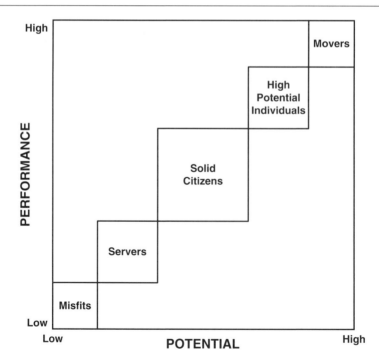

Every organization has its core group of consistently high performers whose potential is also estimated to be high. These are the movers and shakers, the stars that everyone looks up to. They are the ones the organization will want to retain for as long as possible, so that they can eventually provide the leadership for the organization. The percentage of such talent in an organization is relatively small.

Next to these are those considered to be of high potential, whose performance is good and who are currently perceived to have potential to be leaders. They will be groomed to eventually succeed or replace the movers.

The solid citizens are the backbone or the engines that keep the organizational operations running. Their performance is of an acceptable standard, and a few might display higher performance and potential than expected, given the right motivation and effective nurturing on the job. Their skills and knowledge will still need to be upgraded to keep the engine running smoothly and to provide a competitive edge.

There will be a small group who will be there to be led and be told what to do. These are the servers, and they are content where they are and with what they do. A few could be nurtured to join the ranks of the solid citizens. If there is a large group of servers in the organization, its competitive position will be weakened.

Then there are the misfits, who do not belong in the organization because their skills, knowledge, critical attributes and personal values do not fit in with the organization's values and business. Example of misfits are slow-moving people working in a fast-paced business; detached, unfeeling and self-serving people working in care-giving institutions; or opinionated people working in service-oriented businesses.

Misfits could be in an organization because of connections, kinship, through historical carry-over, or the result of a selection error. However, in organizations that can make better use of their skills, knowledge and attributes, they could perform well and excel.

A common pitfall is for an organization to dissipate its energy trying to reform the servers and misfits, to the detriment of others who are more productive and promising. Having such misplaced priorities can place the organization in danger of losing its valued talent.

By and large, talent management deals with people working full-time on the regular payroll; that is, those on contracts of service. There are also contingent talent sources that can be tapped when specialist expertise is needed at short notice. These include consultants, specialist outsource providers, and temporary staff, who are engaged for short durations under contracts for service.

And, of course, there is potential external talent that can be engaged in the long term. That will really be enlarging the scope of talent management.

IDENTIFYING TALENT

What to assess

Two sources provide the input for the talent-management system—the assessment of attributes, and the assessment of potential that follows the annual performance appraisal. The purposes of assessing potential are to identify talent in the organization; and to determine how far that talent can be optimized for mutual benefit.

Any job holder has career aspirations, job satisfaction and lifestyle needs. He also wants to use his talents to meet these needs.

The organization, on the other hand, wants to grow in scope, strength and magnitude. These areas of growth should result in financial growth and long-term sustainability.

A person's acquired skills and knowledge can be used to progress up a professional/technical career ladder. Some also have attributes to assume managerial and leadership roles to enhance the expertise of others within the organization. Such people are thus able to provide more and better products and/or services to the customer or end-user than if they were just professional/technical experts.

Many organizations provide a list of desired attributes for managers to look out for in appraising their direct reports, and by which to gauge their direct reports' strengths and weaknesses based on work interactions and observations.

Other organizations also include input on the incumbent's attributes from those who interact with them both within and outside the organization. Outside parties could include suppliers and customers.

Table 6.1 outlines some of the key attributes organizations look for.

Some of these can be those the organization considers to be core attributes. An example would be integrity, which everyone within the organization must possess. Other attributes are specific to a particular job; for example, the ability to work independently, or the ability to lead or manage other specialist contributors.

How to assess

Before there can be any hope of assessing accurately, there has to be a common and clear understanding of each attribute. Without this, different assessors may have different perceptions and impressions, reducing the validity of the assessments. Having a clear understanding of the intentions and expectations behind each required attribute makes it possible to derive the expected key results areas and key performance indicators that manifest that attribute.

This will reduce disparities in interpretation, especially when we are looking at human qualities. Our own backgrounds and experiences often interfere with our assessment, which is why Table 6.1 incorporates self-assessment, peer-assessment and superior's assessment.

Other, more formal, feedback can be obtained through assessment centers—where personal competencies and attributes are observed and assessed under simulated work activities by a team of trained assessors—and personality-profiling instruments, which are tests to measure personality types or traits. However, the latter may or may not evaluate the attributes that the organization is looking for.

For most organizations, direct observation of the performer in day-to-day work interactions is considered adequate. Perfect measurements of personality traits, types, and attributes seem elusive, and predictability is still an inexact science. However, many organizations do realize that these measures of individual strengths and weaknesses are to ensure company fit and not just job fit.

TABLE 6.1. Assessment of Attributes—A Sample

Observable Attributes	Very Low			Low			Medium			High			Very High		
SP = Supervisor's Assessment SB = Subordinate's Own Assessment PR = Peer's Assessment	SP	SB	PR	SP	SB	PR	SP	SB	PR	SP	SB	PR	SP	SB	PR
Leadership Potential Naturally initiates action needed to reach an objective, solve a problem or make a decision															
Independent Worker Capable of planning, solving problems and making decisions with minimal reliance on management															
Team Player Always has the interest of the group and its objective in mind and willingly															

contributes time, effort and ideas for the sake of the group's achievement			
Abiltiy to Manage Others Capable of getting work done and results through and with others without undue coercion			
Pro-Active Takes responsibility and initiates action to achieve results and get things done without waiting to be told			
Integrity Behaves strictly to a code of ethics, trustworthy, keeps to his word and delivers			

Sourcing Talent

Internal—assessment of potential

Once an organization has determined the skills, knowledge and attributes that it is looking for, the next stage is to identify who among its human resources has got them and the extent to which they have been mastered.

The assessment of potential takes into account the personal attributes that are critical to the organization's business, as well as the performer's past performance, usually over a period of three years or more.

These two major variables are assumed to influence future success in higher-level jobs or positions, because attributes are a person's innate characteristics, and performance is partly the product of the environment (created consciously or otherwise) for people to excel in, related to their attributes. An example of how potential might be assessed is shown in Table 6.2.

TABLE 6.2. Assessment of Potential: Attributes and Performance Matrix

Employee's Attributes	Past Performance (Last 3 Years)		
	Mostly Exceeded Expectations	Mostly Met Expectations	Mostly Did Not Meet Expectations
More organization-relevant strengths than weaknesses	High Potential	High Potential	Considerable Potential
Organization-relevant strengths equal weaknesses	High Potential	Considerable Potential	Low Potential
More organization-relevant weaknesses than strengths	Considerable Potential	Low Potential	Low Potential

To resolve borderline cases, appraisers sometimes take into account the impact of the employee's organization-relevant attributes to the business. This impact is evaluated as Very Critical, Critical and Not So Critical.

For past performance, they consider how good and how consistent the employee's performance has been over the previous three years.

External—recruiting and attracting

Some organizations will only source talent from within, while others will always want to recruit from outside. While recruiting from within tells employees that their performance and/or loyalty are valued, it also runs the risk of putting people in positions for which they are not particularly suited. There is also a danger of fixed mindsets (resulting from having the same people working in the organization for long periods) stifling creativity and new approaches.

Organizations that do not have the internal talent to meet their business needs must recruit from outside. The challenge then is for the new recruits to gain acceptance from their new team mates—direct reports and peers alike. This is where his personal attributes are revealed.

Sourcing external talent is not necessarily limited to recruiting people with experience. The skills and knowledge necessary for business operations can be learned on the job and there are companies that have flourished by making a point of recruiting only fresh graduates and school-leavers with the personal attributes the organization is looking for. This makes business sense, because it is cheaper to train a fresh graduate than to train an experienced worker who has to be employed at a higher pay-scale. It also takes time to change habits of thought and action.

If companies only poached experienced staff from each other, there would be no incentive to train and develop people. This encourages job-hopping, which is detrimental to productivity. In fact, companies that are known for developing their people usually attract a wider talent pool from which to select.

Many seasoned managers consider these to be the factors that make an organization appealing to intending applicants:

- A conducive work environment
- A non-divisive organizational structure
- A seamless work process
- A stable and integrated management system
- A strong and clearly articulated value system

Even then, gathering the best talent does not necessarily translate into organizational success, as talent can only bloom under the right conditions. While talent is undoubtedly the basic ingredient for success, much depends on how it is managed.

Developing Talent

Deployment as an effective development process

Organizations have employed various ways of nurturing talent and these have included both on-the-job and off-the-job training. The former include initiatives like job rotation, while the latter might consist of formalized training, coaching, mentoring, running advanced management programs, as well as arranging attachments and project teams.

A colleague once described to me a logical and pragmatic framework for developing talent based on the premise that on-the-job training and development through deployment is still the best assessment center. This is encapsulated in the mobility-options chart shown in Figure 6.2. The chart is used in conjunction with the promotion and placement decisions, after the assessment-of-potential exercise.

Key positions in the organization are identified in the chart. These are positions that require the professional and technical know-how to deliver products and services to the customer. Without these, the organization cannot meet its customers' expectations.

Just as a hospital needs doctors, a restaurant needs chefs, a university needs lecturers and researchers, and a department

FIGURE 6.2. MOBILITY-OPTIONS CHART

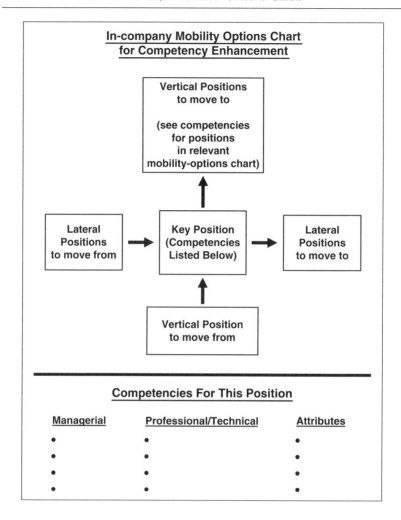

store needs merchandisers and sales personnel, a manufacturing enterprise needs engineers, quality controllers and production personnel.

These core positions need key support functions such as IT, Finance, Accounting, HR, Purchasing and other specializations necessary in a globalized enterprise. These are the benchmark jobs that are used in salary surveys.

For each key position, the managerial and professional/ technical competencies are identified. More importantly, the attributes that will affect the successful performance of the managerial and professional/technical competencies are also identified. Some of these are core organizational and personal values—such as team spirit, good interpersonal relations, and integrity.

TABLE 6.3. CONVENTIONAL INDIVIDUAL PROMOTABILITY AND PLACEMENT ASSESSMENT RECOMMENDATION

Confidential Recommendation (Name of position)			
Promotability	To Managerial Position	Within Same Professional/ Technical Ladder	To Different Professional/ Technical Function
Now			
Within 2–3 years			
In 4–5 years			
Explanation (if any)			

Placement	Remain In Current Position	Lateral Transfer to Better Utilize Abilities	Lateral Transfer for Development	Downgrade to Enable Employee to Perform Better	Terminate
Within the next year					
Within 2–3 years					
Within 4–5 years					
Explanation (if any)					

Others are specific to the position. For sales positions, extro-version and single-mindedness are necessary. For some positions, meticulousness and thoroughness will be critical. For others, a creative and innovative predisposition will be valuable.

The talent managers of this key position will have to identify those that can fill the position and the vertical or promotional possibilities open to the position holder. There are also lateral or placement positions that the key position holder can move to, or where others can move from, for developing competencies and further strengthening attributes.

The Mobility Options Chart can be used in conjunction with the Individual Promotability and Placement Assessment such as that shown in Table 6.3.

In recommending promotability and placement, the recom-mender takes into account the employee's potential, as well as positions available in the organization's succession or renewal plan. This means that an employee with potential sometimes may not be promoted or placed, as there may not be vacancies available.

However, employees with high or considerable potential will normally be shortlisted for consideration for some vacancies. The final selection will depend on how the recommended employee compares with others against the selection criteria.

For *promotability*, the focus is more on *when* rather than *where*. Possible interpretations of the meaning of the various sections of the template are given below.

Promotable Now	This means that the employee is currently under-challenged by the present job, because he has been performing very well in the past three years and shows high potential.
	Any delay may mean losing the employee to another organization that can provide that challenge.
Promotable (2–3 years/ 4–5 years)	This means that even though this employee has displayed considerable potential in performance and personal strengths useful to the organization, he can still learn, develop and find challenge in the current job for the next few years.

For *placement*, the focus is more on *where* rather than *when*.

Remain in Current Position could mean:

There are no positions to promote or transfer the employee to.

There may be positions for the employee to be transferred to, but it is best for this employee to stay and improve performance or acquire more knowledge and skills on the job.

This employee cannot be spared at this time.

Lateral Transfer to Better Utilize Abilities could mean:

The person has considerable or high potential, but there are no positions or vacancies to promote this person to. Will have to job rotate this person as an interim measure to challenge him.

This person's talents are wasted here and can be better used in some other challenging positions.

Lateral Transfer for Development could mean:

The person is performing satisfactorily or well here but can be exposed to other areas to prepare the person for other positions in future.

We want our people to be multi-skilled and have comprehensive knowledge of all aspects of the business.

There are not enough opportunities for the employee to learn on the job in this position.

Downgrade to Enable Employee to Perform Better could mean:

The person has not been doing well in the current position for two years and is not likely to do well in the foreseeable future. Wrong placement here.

The person has been promoted to a level that exceeded his capabilities, and the skills and knowledge that were effective for his previous position are not applicable here. He is displaying incompetence in handling current job.

Terminate could mean:

This position is now redundant.

This person's work attitude, performance, and working relationships are detrimental to the organization's business, and it would take a long time to restore them.

This person cannot be confirmed in his appointment.

Promotability and placement assessments are confidential, as predicting potential is an inexact science, and different assessors predict differently based on their own backgrounds and experiences. Revealing the assessment could either heighten expectations, which may not be fulfilled, or de-motivate or discourage. In any event, people can and do change in different environments and in different periods of their life.

On balance, transparency has to be sacrificed for pragmatic considerations. It is sufficient for the employee to know that his potential to grow with the organization is constantly being updated, and that there is a career path for him. This is in the interests of both the performer and the organization.

Organizations need to deploy and develop talent, but they also need to take into consideration the employee's career preferences, aspirations, work interests, and financial aspirations, recording their discussions with the employee on forms similar to that shown in Table 6.4.

TABLE 6.4. EMPLOYEE CAREER PREFERENCES

Career Preferences	Remain In Present Position	Move to Managerial Position in: _____ (Division/Department)	Move to Professional/ Technical Position in: _____ (Division/Department)
Within the next year			
Within 2–3 years			
In 4–5 years			

Job satisfaction is a major factor in influencing talent retention, yet the employee's personal values, work values, and life interests—which have an impact on job satisfaction—are often overlooked. Personal values include such things as stability, spontaneity, desire to belong, financial or psychological security, self-improvement, self-control, risk-taking, or mental stimulation.

Work values that would have an impact on job satisfaction are factors such as people contact, solitude, variety, creativity, accuracy and precision, authority, influence, decision-making, interaction, competition, and challenge. Life interests, which are crucial for maintaining a healthy work–life balance, might include travel, reading, family activities, concerts and plays, hobbies, music, sports, or other recreational pursuits.

All these influences and preferences together contribute to a person's personality make-up and career satisfaction. They can affect success on the job, especially in a new environment with new managerial styles, new colleagues and work culture. If mismanaged, star performers can turn into non-performers.

TALENT RETENTION

As we saw earlier, an employee's decision to leave is influenced by both external pull factors and push factors from within his current employment. A list of some of the most common reasons for moving are listed in the table below.

TABLE 6.5. FACTORS INFLUENCING A CHANGE OF EMPLOYMENT

Common Pull Factors	Common Push Factors
substantially higher pay	passed over for promotion
better tax-sheltered benefits	unhappy with appraisal rating
greater scope for advancement	limited opportunities for job enlargement
new experiences and challenges	no job security
bigger organization	little or no training provided
opportunities for training	role conflicts and politicking
good organizational climate	daily fire-fighting
well-developed management system	no job satisfaction
better work–life balance	micro management
strong corporate values	work too routine
innovative and cutting-edge work	uncaring superior

Organizations need to pay more attention to internal push factors, rather than just trying to mitigate external pull factors in talent retention. To illustrate this, I gave participants at the Resu training session the following case study to analyze and discuss the various pull and push factors at work here.

SB Associates is in the business of sourcing specialist speakers for themed conferences, conventions, and corporate retreats. The company has a large data bank of such speakers but does not act as their sole agent.

SB Associates has a sales team of experienced client service advisors (CSAs) reporting to a Client Services Manager. The CSAs are paid fixed salaries and variable bonuses based on gross revenue, with no commissions.

For each client, a CSA sources the appropriate specialist speaker or panel of speakers based on a preliminary discussion with the client on their program needs and budgets. When a match is found, the CSA introduces the speaker to the client. They would then design and customize the content.

SB Associates prepares separate contracts between itself and the client and between itself and the speaker.

Since the company's inception, this business model has enabled the CSAs to manage a business within a business. It was designed to authorize them to identify suitable speakers and to negotiate fees, both with the client and the speaker.

Recently, in a bid to grow the business, the management at SB Associates decided to elevate the market position of the business as a top-end provider and to differentiate itself from other agencies providing similar services. Fees had been increased accordingly.

A pool of new specialist resources was identified to augment and eventually to replace the older, more costly, speakers. These new speakers would command lower fees than the seasoned regulars formerly engaged by the organization, thus increasing the profit margins for SB Associates.

Instructions were given to CSAs to use the new, relatively inexperienced but competent speakers, unless the client specifically requested an experienced speaker.

The quality of the matches, which had up till then been handled by the CSAs, also had to be audited. Several fresh MBA holders were hired to perform quality audits, the thinking being that they would bring fresh ideas and different insights.

During the first meeting between a CSA and the client, an auditor had to be present and would later give an opinion on the client's requirements and the issues discussed. The auditors were to review and endorse both the speakers and the customized content they prepared for the client.

Under the new arrangements, fees had to be approved by the Client Services Manager before the CSAs could inform the speakers and the clients.

Within a couple of months of the new business model being implemented, the CSAs resigned one after another; some to start their own businesses, some to join a clients' organization. Others said they just wanted to take a break before looking for another job.

Eventually the Client Services Manager also left.

After reviewing the case in their various groups, the participants shared their observations and reflections, generally basing their comments on their specific areas of expertise.

Ravi, from a recruitment perspective, felt that: "If the purpose of recruiting the auditors was to add value to the business, then some operational experience could have been included in the selection criteria besides freshness and new ideas as newly-minted MBAs. By and large, participants at conferences, conventions, and company retreats are all practitioners. They expect program content to cater to their actual working needs."

From a sales perspective, Sally observed that the CSAs had been "reduced from empowered sales professionals to order-takers, messengers and meeting arrangers." The additional layers of checking, reviewing and auditing that were put in place gave "no measurable value-added to the business processes."

For Frank, the major issue was one of delegation: "It appears that the sales team had all the accountability for results but little authority, and the auditors had all the authority but remote accountability for results. Delegation principles require that authority should be commensurate with the accountabilities expected."

Eugene looked at it from a service-delivery angle, which also had reference to the deployment of talent. "In improving business processes, we try to reduce the number of steps to deliver a product or service to the customer, but in this case, this organization is increasing the steps, delaying response and increasing payroll costs with insignificant value-added to each stage. I don't think it provided an environment conducive for the sales talent to flourish."

Others felt that if the purpose of auditors' reviews and endorsements was to ensure quality control, this was a task that the specialist speakers themselves would be better placed to perform as they were the domain experts and would have their reputations to protect. It was in their interests to meet the client's needs because satisfied clients would use them again.

With regard to the series of resignations, the groups had considerable sympathy with the frustrations experienced by the CSAs, who, they felt, had cause to "feel very redundant." The overall conclusion was that this was "a clear cut case of push factors making it difficult to retain talent."

From this case it is clear that values, organizational structure, and the product/service delivery process can all have an impact on talent management with respect to recruitment, deployment, and retention.

Most business models reflect the value systems of their proponents and have ramifications for the way the organization is structured. Many years ago, when I first started out on a management career, there were two distinct management concepts that held sway. One held that, by and large, workers could not be trusted to put in their best unless controlled, coerced, directed, and checked. Today, we call that micro-managing. The other believed that most people would want to put in a good day's work if entrusted to do so and would exercise self-direction. Today we call that empowerment.

Through an organization's structure may appear sound in concept, in practice there are often role conflicts and blurred authority and accountabilities that cause frustrations and act as push factors. No amount of teambuilding can overcome built-in organizational dysfunctions.

These basic management principles are still being breached in many organizations, despite a plethora of management literature and courses on the latest concepts and techniques.

The bottom line is that retention of talent is not just a matter of being the best paymaster, or providing a suite of the best benefits. Job satisfaction that comes from having a healthy working environment is a potent retention factor in talent management.

In the above case, the talent-management system broke down and failed to retain its proven talent. As a consequence, the company not only incurred recruitment costs but also suffered damage to its image, as well as loss of credibility, goodwill and established personal and business relationships.

TALENT RENEWAL

We'll begin this section by returning to a question that was raised earlier: Is talent management a futile exercise in view of globalization and the increased mobility of talent that it makes possible?

There is an assumption that once recruited, talent should remain with the organization for as long as possible, to recover recruitment and development costs and to derive returns on these investments. This is different from retaining talent for as long as that talent remains effective and relevant to the business of the day.

Talent, as we have seen, is the embodiment of an individual's acquired skills, knowledge and personal attributes that are critical to an organization's deliverables. This also assumes that the individual's personal values are also in harmony with that of the organization—an important consideration in light of all the high-profile corporate malpractices that have surfaced in recent times.

Attitude, skills, knowledge and even attributes may become outdated and their effectiveness can be reduced. A talented person who can produce results independently may not be as effective if new products and services require teamwork to produce results.

How should talent be managed, when there's a need to constantly renew it without having to compete with external pull factors?

The world renowned Vienna Boys' Choir was officially founded in 1924 and it is still singing to appreciative modern audiences worldwide. The Choir consists of boys aged 10 to 14. At any one time, there are about 100 members, divided into four touring choirs.

When the choristers reach the age of 14, their voices are likely to change, yet the high vocal standards of the Choir have to be maintained. This means a constant renewal of these talented choristers is necessary. Recruitment, selection and development to replace those leaving are ongoing activities.

Though the tenure of talent in a business organization is somewhat longer than that in the Choir, the perspective on talent management should be the same. Talent must be recruited, selected, nurtured, deployed, retained, and renewed for as long as that talent is relevant and necessary for the organization.

The old management phrase for talent renewal is "succession planning"—having the right talent in the right place at the right time. Employees see themselves as owners of an asset—their talent—that is being sought. They want to choose where they can invest that asset. If an organization offers them an investment opportunity, then it can be a mutually beneficial and enhancing partnership.

The focus for employees is on where, with whom, and how best to invest their talent. The returns on their investments are not conceived in material terms only. They want to enhance their assets, and derive satisfaction from what they do, in accordance with their personal values and preferred lifestyles.

Therefore, the other old management buzzwords ''career development'' go hand-in-hand with succession planning to facilitate talent renewal. The focus for organizations now is more on finding the right talent to perform the critical jobs that ensure the organization's long-term viability under differing business conditions. This nexus of interests is illustrated in Figure 6.3.

Figure 6.3. Succession Planning and Career Development

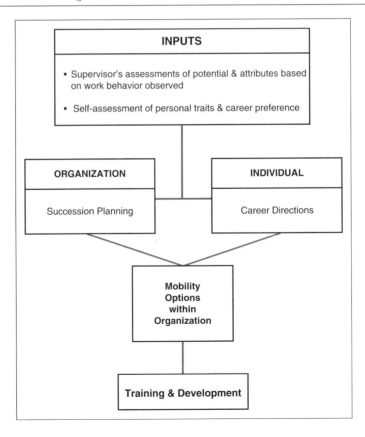

Key Points to Ponder

- A talent-management system is established to balance the long-term career needs of the talent owner and the long-term business needs of the organization. The talent owner wants to optimize his talent and so does the organization.

- Talent management is not confined to the select few high-fliers in an organization.

- Real talent embodies not only skills, knowledge and relevant attributes, but also the talent owner's value system that harmonizes with that of the organization.

- Despite higher talent mobility with globalization, talent management is still a strategic exercise to undertake.

- A comprehensive in-house talent-management system covers identifying, sourcing, developing, retaining and renewing talent for long-term sustainability.

- Talent identification is not an exact science.

- Developing talent is an investment.

- Talent does not need to be retained forever.

- Talent needs to be renewed.

CHAPTER SEVEN

IMPLEMENTING THE RESULTS-MANAGEMENT SYSTEM

Any system is only as good as its implementation

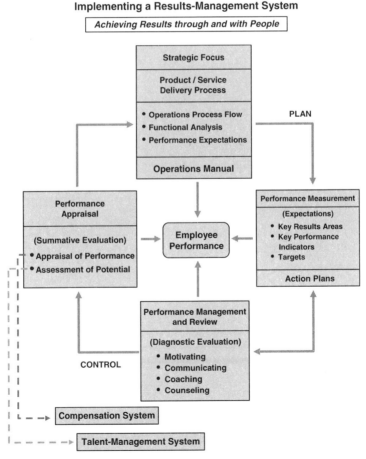

Implementing a Results-Management System

Achieving Results through and with People

© Ong Teong Wan

RECOGNIZING AND ACCEPTING RESISTANCE TO CHANGE

It is something of a truism to say that change is a constant. But it is also true to say that resistance to change is also a constant.

The results-management system we have examined in this book is a people system, and not a paper system. Changing from what has been often perceived as a paper system to a people-centric system poses many challenges to all line managers.

Managing change is critical to the success of any efforts to implement the results-management system, the purpose for which is to improve individual and organizational productivity to address increasing wage costs.

Change-management experts have identified three behavioral impediments to introducing and implementing change: **habits of thought and action; fear of the unknown**; and **vested interests**.

In implementing the results-management system in any organization, the same real issues and concerns related to these impediments are likely to recur: the new system is time-consuming and more difficult to use; we're not sure whether direct reports will accept the new system or whether performance measures will be accurate and complete; results will be harder to achieve and so will my bonus; will I do better or worse under the new system? And so on.

These are genuine concerns. Managing change efforts is not a mechanical textbook exercise and it is helpful if managers can place themselves in their direct reports' position to empathize with their concerns and reservations.

CHANGING HABITS OF THOUGHT AND ACTION

Changing people's habits of thought and action entails having to replace these habits with new ways of thinking and of doing things. The more ingrained the old habits are, the harder it is to change them. The process by which they have become ingrained starts with past experience, which can be pleasant—which will prompt people to want to continue with that experience—or unpleasant or painful—making people want to avoid the experience again. Past experience therefore shapes people's perception of how things should or should not be done. It also causes most people to have fixed assumptions about what they will encounter in the future and thus can get in the way of their accepting something different or new. If, however, their experience of change has been a pleasant one, this may prompt them to accept the new more readily.

Communication and involvement through intensive training in the new—whether this new thing is a product, a service, a concept, a skill or a system—can help overcome resistance. Training experts tell us that people undergo four stages of skills and knowledge acquisition, from awareness, to understanding, insight and mastery, when they learn anything new:

- **Unconscious incompetence**—when they are not aware that they are not understanding or doing things right;

- **Conscious incompetence**—when they are aware of their mistakes in understanding or doing something;

- **Conscious competence**—when they become aware that they understand something and can do it well; and

- **Unconscious competence**—when they can understand and do something well intuitively.[1]

A method commonly used in training sessions to promote awareness is to get people to reflect over their past experiences, pleasant or unpleasant, correct or incorrect. Explanations are given on how they could do things differently, in order to do them better. This leads into the second step and a greater understanding and consciousness of where they have erred. They then will be ready for step three, which is being conscious of where they are right or did right without external feedback. Once they have reached this stage, the learning needs to be reinforced, and it is here, in this fourth stage, that most training programs are generally lacking.

People must realize that it is the constant practice and application of the concepts and skills learned that can enable unconscious competence to take place, for the new concepts and competencies to become ingrained or internalized.

While most training programs have assignments for follow-up application, and end-of-program evaluations, these generally gauge the extent of receptiveness to the new concepts and skills.

After the various projects and assignments have been submitted and reviewed, people tend not think about them much anymore.

For a more effective transfer of training to the workplace, people need to be trained to implement a system; in this case, the results-management system. If the whole organization subscribes to the system, then the attitudes, concepts and skills transmitted will be applied to the workplace for continuing on-the-job training and used till it becomes part of the organizational practice and culture. This will increase the likelihood of creating unconscious competence in the concepts and skills needed to implement and maintain the system.

The components of a results-management system and the competencies needed to implement it are set out in Table 7.1.

TABLE 7.1. COMPETENCIES REQUIRED FOR IMPLEMENTING A
RESULTS-MANAGEMENT SYSTEM

Components of the Results-Management System	Competencies Required
Performance Measurement	Setting Balanced Individual Measures
	Getting Measurement Accepted
Performance Management	Giving Credit
	Constructive Feedback
	Effective Listening
	Handling Conflict
Performance Review	Diagnosing Performance Problems
	Performance Coaching
	Performance Counseling
	Conducting Reviews
Performance Appraisal	Making Balanced Ratings
	Conducting Appraisals
Compensation System	Evaluating Jobs
	Using Salary Survey Reports
	Paying for Performance

Talent-Management System	Identifying Talent
	Attracting Talent
	Developing Talent
	Retaining Talent
	Renewing Talent

Companies obviously want their investment in training to pay off and Figure 7.1 illustrates how returns on investment in training could be derived.

FIGURE 7.1. TRANSFER OF TRAINING TO ACHIEVE UNCONSCIOUS COMPETENCE

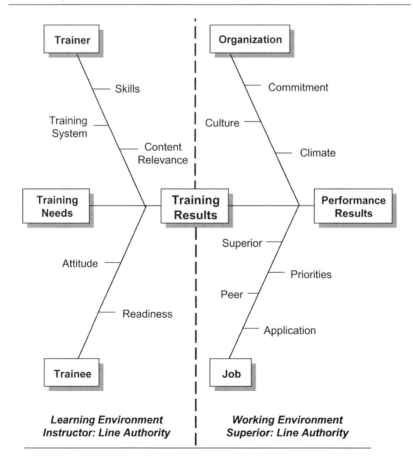

From this, it becomes clear that off-the-job training can create awareness, understanding, and the likelihood of acceptance of new concepts and skills, which is often revealed in the reactions of the participants in the end-of-program evaluation.

After the training, the skills and concepts learned have to be applied in the work environment to bring that learning to a state of unconscious competence. These applications must be reinforced by organizational commitment, which determines the organizational climate to encourage continual practice.

In the workplace itself, if everyone learns the same system, concepts, and skills, and the immediate superior accords priority to their implementation, this will serve to encourage regular application and practice.

Concepts, when applied often enough, lead to greater insights. Skills, if practiced often enough, lead to intuitive actions. Once this stage is reached, the old habits of thought and action would have been changed.

Training is usually seen as a means to an end. In this instance, training helps to bring about change, by helping people to look at things and do things differently.

REDUCING FEAR OF THE UNKNOWN

Another factor militating against change is fear of the unknown. This is often compounded by a fear of failure or of looking stupid if the concepts and skills are wrongly applied. To overcome such fears and to ensure success, it may be necessary to take small, incremental steps in implementing change. Celebrate the little successes. Success begets success as it breeds confidence.

An effective strategy is to have pilot runs of small parts of the system progressively. De-bug them, make them work, and then move on to the next part of the system. Alternatively, pilot the whole system with the department or group that is most receptive, and ensure that it succeeds. The pilot project can be run in parallel with the current system.

Once the pilot project is successful, celebrate it and disseminate the learning as a model for emulation, to spur on others who may be ambivalent about it. If possible, leave the most resistant groups to the last.

This may take some time but the entire results-management system is made up of many sub-systems, each of which requires a number of core competencies to be mastered in order for it to be implemented well.

Transition in change management can be likened to the trapeze artist who has to take that leap of faith. He has to let go of the current handle and lunge forward to grab the next handle coming towards him. Rushing or pushing him forward could prove fatal.

Taking Care of Vested Interests

Vested interests come in various forms. They can be simple human self-interest, self-preservation, or self-protection. They need to be addressed as they can impede any change initiative, but they can also aid the change if certain self-interests are addressed.

As shown in Figure 7.2, about 20 percent of employees in any organization will be dead-set against a change, as they will perceive the change to be detrimental to them. Another 20 percent will strongly favor the change, as they see immediate benefits to them, or they have not been benefiting under the current system. The remaining 60 percent will be ambivalent, sitting on the fence to

Figure 7.2. Distribution of Vested Interests Within an Organization

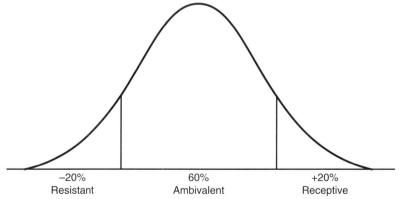

| −20% | 60% | +20% |
| Resistant | Ambivalent | Receptive |

see what happens. This critical mass has to be influenced for any significant change to come about.

Obviously, these will differ according to the type of organization and the type of change being sought. To ascertain the actual distribution of vested interests within a specific organization, focus groups can be formed to discuss and gather concerns and issues regarding the intended changes. These focus groups will act as the organization's eyes and ears, to find out what people need, fear to lose or need to protect.

Then, win-win solutions must be found. If win-win solutions are not immediately available, trade-offs can be considered (if a person is going to lose something in the compensation system, for example, a substitute in the talent-management system might be an acceptable trade-off).

Line managers will also have a major role to play in this because most concerns and anxieties are best learned unobtrusively in day-to-day interactions between superior and direct report, when people are less guarded.

Organizing for Implementation

Four groups of people are involved in the implementation stage:

1. Top Management—set the tone and provide the leadership to implement the system.

   Their commitment is critical for success. The commitment level should not be lower than that required for implementing other business-enhancing initiatives such as ISO standards, IT systems, accounting systems, and so on.

2. Advocates or Drivers—a steering committee comprising senior line and staff personnel to support, plan, and review the implementation initiatives.

3. Activists—line managers who plan and manage the operational issues in implementing the system.

4. Employees—who receive, accommodate, and adjust to the changes.

This is not an HR project, but a company project. There must be ownership by everyone in the organization, but HR will play the role of facilitator, and line managers will play the role of implementers. Details of their respective roles are set out in Table 7.2.

DEVELOPING AN ACTION PLAN

A possible action plan to support the implementation could be done in three phrases:

Phase 1: Initiation

- Explain the need for change to all employees.
- State the expected outcomes.
- Explain the impact of change—what will change, who will be affected, what needs to be overcome, what needs to be retained.
- Establish and explain roles of line and support departments.
- Introduce steering committee comprising senior management.

Phase 2: Transition

- Publicize the system and draw up action plans.
- Train all employees.
- Train and certify in-house facilitators and instructors.
- Achieve small successes—launch pilot projects.
- Evaluate milestone results and fine-tune progressively.
- Celebrate mini-successes and recognize all contributions.
- Create a positive buzz to surround the change.
- Keep communications open and inform people of progress.
- Form focus groups to get people involved and obtain feedback.
- Address concerns, tap ideas, and share results.
- Follow up regularly and consistently with key implementers.
- Keep everyone in the loop to help them take the leap of faith.

TABLE 7.2. RESPECTIVE ROLES OF HR AND LINE MANAGEMENT

Parts of the Results-Management System	Role of the HR Function	Role of Line Management
Performance Measurement	Train	Set targets with direct reports
	Audit performance measures established	Achieve understanding and acceptance of performance measures
Performance Management	Train	Apply skills
	Arrange sharing of learning experiences	Share learning experiences
Performance Review	Schedule	Apply skills
Performance Appraisal	Monitor	Share learning experiences
	Train	Conduct reviews and appraisals
	Consolidate appraisal returns	
Compensation System	Coordinate job evaluations	Communicate compensation system to direct reports
	Conduct salary surveys	
	Develop pay-for-performance criteria	Prepare salary budgets
Talent-Management System	Coordinate implementation of system	Identify talent
		Develop talent
		Retain talent
		Renew talent
Implementing the Results Management System	Co-ordinate	Implement

Phase 3: Consolidation

- Evaluate the results of change.
- Announce results and follow-up actions to be taken.
- Monitor and fine-tune system.
- Hold regular de-briefing and update sessions.
- Hold formal departmental ceremonies to celebrate successes.
- Hold formal celebration of project completion.

Acting on the initiatives suggested above is recognizing and working on the "driving forces" and "resisting forces" which most managers have learned from Kurt Lewin's well-known Force Field Analysis to bring about change.

Finally, a system is often held together and is inter-dependent with several sub-systems. Any malfunction in one can affect the proper functioning of the whole system. This applies to the implementation of the results-management system as well. Only committed organizational leadership can bring about an efficient and effective implementation of such a system.

Key Points to Ponder

- A system is only as good as its implementation.
- Even though the results-management system is a people system and not a paper system, resistance to change must still be managed.
- Three major impediments to change have to be recognized and managed: habits of thought and of action; fear of the unknown; and the vested interests of people affected by the change.

(*continued*)

- To change habits of thought and of action, we can take a leaf from the training profession, which creates awareness of a need, enables people to recognize their ineffective habits, and to practice and internalize their effective habits.
- Individuals who change habits need to be reinforced by the environment they return to.
- Informal communication can help uncover and mitigate fear of the unknown.
- To attend to vested interests that can impede change, it is necessary to find out what these vested interests are and seek win-win solutions.
- The roles of everyone in the organization have to be spelt out, so that each group or individual will implement the action plan as a team, pulling in the same direction.

ENDNOTE

1. Adapted from, Howell, William S., *The Emphatic Communicator*, Wadsworth Publishing Company, 1982, pp. 29–33.

INDEX

A

above target, 99, 100, 103, 106
accountabilities, xvii, 144, 145
accountability for results, 26–30, 86,
    114, 144
achieving results, xxxi, 1, 11, 39, 93,
    111, 125, 149
action plan, 1, 11, 25–26, 28, 39, 40, 89,
    93, 104, 111, 125, 149, 157–160
activists, 156
actual results, 6, 7, 31, 32, 42, 74, 94,
    95, 96, 98
advisory role, 143
advocates or drivers, 156
Allen, Louis A., 95
annual increments, 8
annual performance appraisal
    discussion, 107–108
appraisal (see performance appraisal,
    annual appraisal)
appraisal ratings, xx, xxvi, xxviii, 8, 85,
    88, 109
appraisal system, xix, xxi, xxv, xxvii–
    xxix, xxxi, xxxii, 6, 94, 98, 106, 123
appraiser, xx, xxi, xxiv–xxviii, 6, 102, 135
aptitude, 48, 127
assessment centers, 126, 131, 136, 141
assessment of attributes, 130, 132
assessment of potential, xi, 8, 95, 126,
    130, 134
attitude, xx, 16, 47, 48, 61, 70–72, 76,
    80, 85, 86, 95, 146, 152
attract and retain, 3, 118
attract talent, 3, 113, 153

attributes, 7, 127, 129–132, 134, 135,
    138, 139, 146
attributes and performance, 134
authority, 20, 86, 115, 142, 144, 145

B

balanced rating, 152
balanced targets, 16
barriers to communication, 57, 78, 83
base pay increases, 121
base salary increment, xxxi
behavior, xix, xxi, xxiv, xxv, xxvii, 6, 7,
    43, 45, 47, 51, 77, 81, 82, 84, 86,
    96, 150
behaviorally anchored rating scale
    (BARS system), xxi, xxi, xxvii, 6, 96
below target, 99, 100
benchmark jobs, 115, 137
bunched ratings, 26
business development process, 3
"busy" work, 86, 120
buzzwords, 147

C

career development, 127, 147
career preferences, 141, 147
cashflow, 24
challenging and achievable targets,
    21–24
changing habits of thought and action,
    150–154
collective agreements, 118
commissions, 15, 33, 35, 121, 143
company fit, 131

compensation system, xxxii, 3, 7–8, 86, 114, 117, 118, 123, 126, 156
competency enhancement, 137
competitiveness, xxxi, 41, 114, 117–119
components of pay increases, 114, 121
components of the results-management system, 152
conducting salary surveys, 119–120
conscious competence, 151–154
conscious incompetence, 151
consolidation phase, 159
constructive feedback, 6, 49, 51, 53, 71, 75, 76, 79, 83
contract for service, 130
conventional appraisal system, xxv, xxxi
coordinating role, 158
corporate governance, 66
corporate values, 4, 8, 97, 106, 107, 121, 122
corrective action, 51, 79, 87
cost-of-living increase, 121
cost-effective, 15, 17, 35, 121
culture (corporate, organizational), 2, 24, 43, 50, 69, 106, 121, 142, 152

D
data collection, 119
defensive statements, 79
defensiveness, 31, 51, 53, 75, 77, 78, 79, 83, 84, 85, 107
deployment (of talent), 136, 144, 145
descriptors, xxviii, 94
develop talent, 141
diagnostic evaluation, 88, 91, 95, 109
differentiation, xv, 70, 94
difficulties (with appraisal forms), xx, xxi, xxiv, xxxii, 71, 89, 101, 107
direct observation, 131
direct reports, 7, 21, 24, 28, 29, 43, 49, 52–55, 59, 65–69, 71–76, 79, 81, 84, 85, 94, 121, 130, 135, 150, 156
distribution of talent, 128
distribution of vested interests, 155, 156

domain experts, 145
downgrade, 138, 140
Drucker, Peter, xxviii
dysfunctional teams, xvi

E
effective listening, 54–59, 71, 76, 79
effective management of payroll, 113
effectiveness, xxi, 2, 3, 15–17, 18, 20, 38, 85, 95, 101, 102, 113, 146
effectiveness of payroll, 113
effectiveness results, xxi, 2, 15–18, 146
efficiency, 15–18, 20, 38, 85, 101, 102
efficiency results, 102
emotional responses to salary, 15
empathy, 81
employee commitment, xvii, 59
employee loyalty, 59, 135
employees, xxii, xxvi, xxxi, 3–6, 8, 16, 19, 31, 32, 35, 52, 59, 67, 69, 71, 82, 112, 113, 116–119, 121, 126, 134, 135, 138–142, 146, 147, 155–157
ensuring productivity, 120
environment for people, xviii
establishing internal equity, 114
establishing performance measures, 7, 14, 17, 32, 38
establishing salary ranges, 115–118
evaluating past performance, 134, 135
evaluation of performance, xiii, xxxii
evaluation system, 106, 115
expectations, xi, xvii, xx, 13–17, 19, 46, 48, 49, 51, 75, 77, 79, 82, 91, 102, 106, 131, 136, 141
expected results, 7, 8, 27, 28, 31, 40, 95–98, 103, 106, 126
experienced people, 97
external competitiveness, 114, 118, 119
external customer, xviii, 14, 21, 38
external pull factors, 142, 143
external talent, 130, 135

F
far above target, 99, 100
far below target, 99, 100

fear of the unknown, 150, 154, 160
five-point scale, xxix, 97
fixed costs, xxxi, 113
forced ranking, xxv, xxvi, 96
formalized testing, 136
four phases of learning competency, 151
functional results area, 98, 99, 102

G

getting measurement accepted, 30–32
giving credit, 45–49, 71, 76, 79
green-circled jobs, 117

H

habits of action, 150
habits of thought, 150, 154
handling conflict, 60, 62, 63, 65, 79
high potential, 126, 128, 129, 139, 140
hiring policies, 118
Howell, William S., 160
HR function, 158
human impact, 17, 20, 101, 102
human reaction, 16, 17, 19, 20, 27, 33
human subjectivity, 101

I

identifying talent, 130–133
implementing results-management system, xi, 1, 11, 39, 93, 111, 125, 149, 150, 152
importance of periodic results reviews, 42, 87–91, 102
impressionistic evaluations, 97, 106
in-company mobility options, 137
increasing wage costs, xxxi, 150
ineffective management of payroll, 113
initiation phase, 157
integrity, 131, 138
intellectual capital, 8, 41, 121
intended outcomes, 121
inter-functional working relationships, xviii, 30
internal customer, 21, 27, 38
internal equity, 18, 114

internal push factors, 42, 143
internal talent, 135
ISO, xvii, 156

J

job descriptions, xvii, 36, 114
job evaluation, 18, 114
job evaluation committee, 18, 114, 158
job factors, 114
job grade, 115, 120
job knowledge, xx, xxiii
job satisfaction, 42, 130, 141, 145
job titles, 115, 116
judgment, xxiv, xxvi, 35, 96–98

K

key considerations in salary surveys, 119
key elements of a compensation system, 114
key performance indicators, 5, 19–21, 40, 131
key position competencies, 40, 41, 152
key results areas, 3, 5, 14, 17–20, 27, 30, 31, 33, 40, 41, 98, 107, 131
knowledge, xx, xxi, 3, 29, 42, 47, 48, 63, 65, 69–71, 95, 114, 121, 127–130, 134, 135, 146, 151

L

lateral or placement positions, 137, 139
lateral transfer, 138, 140
learning curve, 48
level of difficulty, 90, 101–103, 109, 115,
level of importance, 100, 102, 103, 105
Lewin, Kurt, 159
life interests, 141, 142
line management, 158
line manager, xi, xiii, xiv, xviii, xix, xx, xxi, xxiv, xxviii, xxxi, xxxiii, 2, 7, 8, 13, 15, 29, 36, 40, 65, 66, 88, 92, 94, 114, 123, 124, 126, 150, 156, 157
line roles, 158
long-term viability, 3, 113, 147
low potential, 128, 134

M

Mager, Robert F., 92
management functions, 28, 41
management work, 102
managerial functions, 36, 37, 40–42, 92, 98
managing change, 150
managing for commitment, 6, 39, 42–45, 52
managing for compliance, 6, 52, 62
maximum base pay, 115
maximum of salary range, 116
measurement of personality traits, 131
merit increases, 118
mid-career professionals, 141
mid-point base pay, 115, 116
mid-point of salary range, 116
minimum base pay, 115
minimum of salary range, 116
misfits, 128, 129
mission statement, 23
mobility options chart, 136, 137, 139
movers and shakers, 128, 129
multi-rater feedback, xxviii–xxx

N

non-discriminatory, 118
non-performers, 142

O

objective computation, 96
objectivity and subjectivity, 96
observable attributes, 132
off-the-job-training, 136, 154
on target, 99, 100, 103, 106
on-the-job training, 29, 69, 121, 136, 152
operational procedures, xvii
organizational values, xvi
organizing for implementation, 156–157
organizational productivity, 150
organization structure, xvii, 41
organization-relevant attributes, 135
outsource, xviii, 4, 15, 18, 130
overall performance rating, 103, 108

overall results, 7, 26, 28, 99, 100, 103
owners of an asset, 146

P

paper system, 87, 150, 159
paradigm shift, xxxi
pay increases, 114, 121
paying above the maximum, 117
paying for performance, 3, 18, 114, 118, 120–124, 126, 152
paying for seniority, 118
paying for the job, 3, 114–118, 124
paying market rates, 3, 114, 118–120, 124
payroll costs, 113, 144
payrolls, 113, 130
peer assessment, 131
people system, 87, 150, 159
perceptions, xxi, 27, 57, 68, 88, 100, 113, 115, 123, 131, 150
performance, xxix, xxxi, 5, 7, 11, 17, 32, 39–92, 93–96, 107, 120, 128, 134
performance and talent 41
performance appraisal, xxix, xxxi, 3, 7, 90, 93–108
performance coaching, 42, 69–71, 74, 152
performance counseling 70, 80–82, 83, 86, 152
performance management, xiv, xxxii, 3, 5–7, 39–92, 128, 152, 158
performance measurement, xxxi, 3, 5, 11–37
performance rating, 102, 103, 123
performance review, 6, 7, 42, 152, 158
performer's reaction, 97
periodic results review, 42, 87–91, 95, 96, 101–102, 104
personal values, 129, 138, 141, 146, 147
personality profiling, 131
perverted outcomes, 32, 121
Pipe, Peter, 92
pitfalls, xxx, 32–34, 68, 77, 87, 129
placement, 138–141
point values, 114–116
position in salary range, 122, 123

potential, 128, 134
preventive action, 26, 51, 95
probation period, 81, 117
process, 17, 27, 74, 82, 83, 95
process of establishing performance measures, 17
product/service-delivery system, 4
productive work 120
productivity, xi, xix, xxxi, 2, 8, 16, 40, 54, 60, 113, 118, 120, 150
professional/technical functions, 36, 40, 98, 138
promotability, 138, 139, 141
promotable to the next grade, 117
pull factors, 42, 63, 118, 142, 143
push factor, 42, 63, 86, 118, 142, 143, 145

Q
quality control, 144
quantified approach, 114

R
recruiting and attracting, 135
red-circled jobs/rate, 117
relative importance, 101
relative weighting, 36, 37, 102, 103
reliability, xxiv, xxxii, 106, 115, 119
renewal of talent, 146–147
resistance to change, 150
resistances and symptoms, 75, 77
resourcefulness, xx, xxii, xxvi, 127
results areas, 3, 5, 17–20, 27, 30, 31, 33, 40, 41, 98, 99, 103, 106, 107, 131
results-management system, xii, xxviii, xxxii, xxxii, 1, 4, 5, 7, 8, 11, 39, 41, 42, 87, 93, 94, 106, 111, 114, 125, 149–159
retain talent, xxxii, 3, 8, 113, 145
retention of talent, 145
return on investments, 29
returns on investment in training, 153
reward system, xxxi, 122
rewarding performance, 9
right place, 125, 146
right talent, 125, 146, 147

right time, 80, 125, 146
role conflicts, xvii, 30, 142, 145

S
salary budget, 122, 158
salary increase guide, 123
salary policy line, 119–120
salary ranges, 115–118, 120, 122
salary surveys, 18, 19, 119, 137
self-appraisal, 6, 94, 107, 108
self-assessment, 131
servers, 128, 129
setting targets, 6, 14, 15, 21, 28, 36, 40, 90
seven-point scale, 97
skills, 69
SMART criteria, 14
soft questions, 81, 82, 84
solid citizens, 128, 129
sound compensation system, 114, 118
sourcing for talent, 134, 135
specific results, xvii, 13, 14, 20, 21, 27
split functions, 115
star performers, 142
steering committee, 156, 157
strategic focus, xi, 1, 3, 4, 11, 39, 93, 111, 125, 149
structure, xvi, xvii, xix, 2, 41, 127, 145
subjective assessment, 96
succession planning, 7, 126, 127, 146, 147
summative evaluations, 1, 3, 8, 11, 39, 42, 93, 94, 102, 107, 111, 125, 126, 149
superior assessment, 131
superior–subordinate relationships, 73, 74
supply and demand for talent, 119
support roles, 3, 21, 137
system implementation, 98

T
talent (identify, attract, develop, retain, renew), 126
talent (what it comprises), 126–127
talent management, 8, 41, 94, 126–130, 145, 146

talent-management system,
  1, 3, 7, 8, 11, 39, 93, 94, 111,
  125–127, 130, 145, 148, 149, 153,
  156, 158
talent owners, 127, 148
talent renewal, 146–147
team spirit, xxiv, 60, 121, 127, 138
teambuilding retreats, xviii, 145
teamwork, xx, xxiii, xxiv, xxvi, 16, 30,
  53, 106, 146
terminate, 138, 140
360-degree appraisal/feedback,
  xxix–xxx
three-point scale, 97
tone from the top, 2, 24
traits, xx, xxvi, xxvii, xxix, 127, 131
transfer of training, 29, 152, 153
transition phase, 157
turn-offs, 43, 44, 67
turn-ons, 44, 55, 67

U
unconscious competence,
  151–154
unconscious incompetence, 151
understanding and acceptance, 22, 30,
  40, 52, 74, 83, 94, 97, 108, 119

unquantified approach, 114
usefulness of periodic results reviews,
  102

V
validity and reliability, xxiv, xxxii,
  115, 119
value system, xvi, xviii, 2, 40, 72, 106,
  136, 145, 148
value-added, 3, 4, 144
values, xvi–xviii, 4, 8, 35, 57, 58,
  62–63, 106–107, 114, 115, 117,
  121, 122, 124, 129, 138, 141–142,
  145–147
variable bonuses, 8, 107, 113, 114,
  121–123, 143
variable costs, 8, 113, 114
vertical or promotional position, 139
vested interest, 12, 62, 150, 155, 156
viability of the company, 113
Vienna Boys' Choir, 146

W
willing and able, 47, 51, 70,
  127
work-life balance, 121, 142
work values, 141